The Mystery of Judas

Kerry Jehanne-Guadalupe

The Mystery of Judas
All Rights Reserved
Copyright © 2021 Kerry Jehanne-Guadalupe
Cover © 2025 Kerry Jehanne-Guadalupe.

Journey of the Phoenix Publishing
https://www.journeyofthephoenix.org
journeyofthephoenixbooks@gmail.com

ISBN: 9798589027112

This book may not be reproduced, transmitted, or stored in whole or in part by any means, including graphic, electronic, or mechanical without the express written consent of the publisher except in the case of brief quotations embodied in critical articles and reviews.

For Judas and His Sacred Sacrifice

Table of Contents

Acknowledgments II

Part 1: Introduction 1

   A Contemplation 1

   Navigating and Working in Levels of Consciousness 3

   Soul Fragments 5

   Truth 8

   The Structure of This Book 11

Part 2: Journeying with Judas 13

   A Random Thought 13

   From Hell to the House of the Lord 14

   Cutting the Unbiblical Cord 16

   Banished to Hell as Judas 21

   The Dawn That is Awakening 27

   Motherly Love 28

   Embedded in the Truth is a Power 29

   The Bedroom Tomb 31

   Roc-a-Sha 33

   Stigmata 34

   The Egg of Earth and Heaven 36

Altered at the Altar	39
A Journey of Surrender and Release	42
Healing the Heart of Judas	44
A Reunion with Creator	48
Judas's Life as Sacred and Holy	51
The Mother of a Savior	54
What Judas was Born to Do	56
From Fragmented to King	57
Cleaning up Hell	61
Turtle	63
Death of Judas	65
Freeing the Souls who Killed Judas	67
Black Sheep Birthing Sacred Lambs	69
Deliverance Through Betrayal	70
Laurels	74
True God and False Gods	78
Judas Christ is Born	91
Moving Statues	94
I Am Judas - I Am Mother	95
Entering the Heavenly Realms	102
Embodying Judas	105

A Tear in the Universe 106
Witnessing the Glory, Not the Story 108
Ark of the Covenant 110
Five White Petals 112
Judas and Magdalene 113
Jesus's Love and Judas's Medicine 114
The Medicine of the Middle 116

Part 3 – Reflections 121
The Power of a Story 121
The Gospel of Judas 122
Historical Judas 127
Fabricated, Heretical, and Hidden in the Dark 131
The Power of Myth 133
The Bare Truth; Cross to Bear 137
Thirteenth God 138
The Curse 142
The Martyrdom of Judas 145
Sacrifice and Sacredness 149
Reorganization of the Cosmos 150
The Infinity of Judas 152
Judas and the Unfinished Tikkun 155

Holy Hell 159

The Star of Judas 163

Friday the 13th, Holy Days of Remembrance 166

Discerning Light from Illusion 166

Judas as a Guide in the Pursuit of Truth 169

If the Crucifixion Never Happened............................. 170

Part 4: The Mirror and the Sword................................ 175

The Nature of Authentic Facilitation 176

Jesus as a Facilitator: The Sword of Truth................... 181

Judas as a Facilitator: The Mirror of Betrayal 185

The Scapegoat and the Shadow 186

Judas as an Authentic Facilitator 189

Judas's Kiss: The Mirror of Humanity's Betrayal 192

The Price of True Facilitation 193

Rewriting the Myth and Updating the Archetype 194

Jesus, the Timeless Facilitator 196

Judas, the Unseen Facilitator 197

Come to Jesus: Come to Judas 199

Being Facilitated by Judas... 200

Part 5: The CrissCross.. 206

Works Cited 230

Acknowledgments

For Krishna. I am deeply grateful for your loving and steadfast encouragement while I journeyed through complex and unfamiliar multidimensional terrain. Thank you for listening to the details of my visions as they occurred as well as supporting me as I worked to articulate my mysterious experiences in writing for this book.

For dear friends, especially Jae, Kristen, Laura, Susan, and Sierra who held space for me as I navigated the complexities of my experiences with Judas. I sincerely appreciate your unwavering support and loving hearts.

For all those who have spoken their truth, especially when it contradicts conventional thought and what we have been taught to believe as true. Thank you for being an inspiration to me. Simply by being you, you helped me find the courage to speak my truth as well.

Part 1: Introduction

A Contemplation

Thank you for joining me.

When perplexing and mystifying visions of Judas Iscariot started to come to me in my dreams, I didn't know what to do with the information other than to receive and let be. Two years after the initial dreams, I had numerous multidimensional journeys that were shamanic in nature. In one of the journeys, Spirit asked if I would be willing to write a book about Judas, to which I agreed without hesitation. This book is the manifestation of that request.

In the following pages, I share my visions as they occurred and offer my reflections as an unsolved mystery. I do my best to detail the information I received and pray I do justice in articulating my experience of Judas in a way that best serves his essence and anyone who reads these pages. At the same time, I acknowledge that a mere book cannot illuminate the multidimensionality and complexity of what all of this possibly means.

Though I have had numerous visions, I feel I have sensed, witnessed, and experienced only a sliver of Judas's true essence, a being that I have come to know as powerfully mystical, angelic, and holy. I feel I have perceived only part of the mystery Judas embodies, a piece that stands well outside of traditional thought and one that I only scratched the surface of understanding. I believe that other people hold additional elements of Judas's mystery and wonder what beauty, power, and knowledge could arise if the pieces come together. I pray for our paths to intersect as Judas might hold a key to heralding a shift in consciousness and the furtherment of our human, planetary, and galactic evolution.

I do not claim that my visions represent the absolute truth of Judas. In this manuscript, I share my journeys and then ponder what they revealed. I work with the images and information as they came to me and wonder if they were accurate, how is the information meaningful to our human existence, and what can be understood or learned? For example, some information revealed in my visions was that: Judas was killed, he did not commit suicide; there was no betrayal, but an agreement; and Judas resides in the high reaches of heaven as a powerful, divine, and loving being. Instead of rejecting the information because it does not align with conventional thought, I work with the visions and contemplate, if this is true: what is the significance of the information; why was a false narrative created; why was the truth hidden; what could all this mean within the context of the mysteries of the heavens; what is Judas's truth; and much more.

I do not claim my visions as the ultimate truth but as a gateway to contemplating what might be incomprehensible while still in form. I offer my thoughts and contemplations as possibilities, not as fact. I have many unanswered questions about the purpose and relevance of Judas's mystical existence, and I offer these questions up to Creator as a deep and life-long prayer. I rest in faith that my prayer will be answered in some realm of time and space. I do not offer this book as part of the contentious debate related to Judas, but instead, I offer this book to you as a form of prayer and as a heart-based contemplation.

I invite you to journey, pray, and contemplate with me in the mystery of Judas.

With love,
Kerry Jehanne-Guadalupe

Navigating and Working in Levels of Consciousness

The information that I received about Judas came through dreams, multidimensional journeys, and one past-life regression. The journeys were shamanic in nature where I was able to access non-ordinary realms of consciousness. I entered and navigated diverse levels of consciousness that were previously totally foreign and somehow felt familiar. The totality of what I experienced cannot be explained. The how and why of these experiences remain as questions.

Within both the dream state and the journeys, there was an active rather than passive nature to the visions where Spirit asked me to participate in a process. Within distinct levels of consciousness, specific work needed to be done, information conveyed, or someone needed support in healing. Sometimes the other places and dimensions I traveled to were earth-based, only in another time period. Other times the journeys had a heavenly nature, and sometimes the work Spirit was asking me to do required me to go deep into the depths of darkness.

In many visions, I appeared as Judas. In a few, I was his mother. Was I actually them? I don't feel I was either Judas or his mother, as it felt more like temporary embodiments of them. I connected to certain levels of consciousness as either Judas or his mother, and in these embodiments, I could access specific energies and information that were necessary to be either transmuted or understood.

Many journeys evoked an inexplicable mixture of thoughts and emotions as I knew the experiences and information were directly related to Judas. At the same time, I wondered how this could be? I knew this was not mere archetypal work I was personally doing and that the information I received was connected to Judas himself. If this was not a metaphor or archetypal work, then what?

Was this a contract or an agreement I had with the essence of Judas? If so, why? What was the purpose of the information, and why was it coming through me? I knew this was not a metaphor for me to decode, and at the same time, it was hard not to question.

In one of the journeys, I asked Spirit if this was all a metaphor, even though deep in my heart I knew it was not. After I asked Spirit, I heard the word metaphor broken down into 'meta' and 'poor.' I understood this to mean the information I was receiving was in no way a metaphor. It was 'poor' thinking to link sacred information to a metaphor or an archetypal work. Spirit emphasized, "Meta, meta, meta! Focus on the meta!" Meta is a Greek prefix with several uses and meanings such as comprehensive, transcending, after, and beyond. When combined with words, meta often signifies change, transformation, or alteration, such as metamorphic, metaphysics, and metabolic. When guided to focus on the 'meta,' I understood to focus on a combination of many of the above meanings and usages: focus on the more comprehensive understanding of Judas that transcends traditional knowledge; go beyond what is currently understood; allow the 'meta' information to bring transformation and change.

Soul Fragments

A number of people have offered possible explanations for my experience. One explanation came from my friend, Kathy. She suggested that as our spirits journey toward incarnation, they may pass through the etheric realm of another being. If this occurs, we can take on aspects of that soul. Kathy differentiates between carrying an element of another being and being the actual reincarnation of that soul. I have met others who have had similar experiences and describe their connection to a being as carrying a spark or fragment of the other soul. The sense of responsibility that comes with this varies from person to person.

The concept of unhealed energies and soul fragments moving across time and space is deeply embedded in shamanic and mystical traditions worldwide. Many Indigenous traditions, from the Americas to Siberia and Mongolia, teach that trauma or profound emotional experiences can cause soul fragmentation. This occurs when part of the soul or consciousness "splits off" as a survival mechanism, protecting itself from pain. Such fragmentation often arises from betrayal, grief, or violent death—circumstances that leave behind unresolved energy.

It is thought that these fragments do not simply disappear; they remain trapped in certain timelines, locations, or even within the energetic fields of other beings. Some may linger in the energetic imprint of a place, as seen in ancestral trauma. Others may enter the collective unconscious or attach to individuals who resonate with them—those who, knowingly or unknowingly, help facilitate their healing.

Tibetan Buddhism describes the *bardo* states—intermediate realms where consciousness exists between death and rebirth. Souls that remain bound by attachments, fear, or confusion can become fragmented or lost. Certain Buddhist practices, such as *phowa* (the transference of consciousness) and prayers for the dead, aim to guide these souls toward enlightenment.

Jewish mysticism also offers insight into the idea of fragmented souls. Some Kabbalistic traditions teach that souls do not always reincarnate as whole entities but may be distributed across multiple individuals. A person might not be the full reincarnation of another but could carry an aspect of a soul's unresolved work. The concept of *ibbur* describes a positive form of soul merging, where a soul fragment temporarily joins another for healing or spiritual growth. In some interpretations, soul fragments temporarily attach to individuals as part of a greater cosmic process of soul repair (*Tikkun HaNefesh*).

Some esoteric interpretations of reincarnation suggest that souls take on karmic imprints or fragments from past lives or other entities as part of their evolutionary journey. In Hindu and New Age thought, unresolved energies may persist across lifetimes, and beings may absorb aspects of others' unhealed energies as a form of karmic service. Karmic debts are believed to extend not only across an individual's own lifetimes but also through interactions with others connected to those unresolved energies.

Gnostic interpretations offer yet another perspective, particularly regarding figures like Judas. Some Gnostic traditions view Judas not as a betrayer but as a necessary catalyst for spiritual evolution. If Judas's energy remains unresolved in the collective consciousness, it may seek integration through those attuned to it. In this view, individuals who carry fragments of his energy serve as a bridge between *what was* and *what is becoming*, between past misunderstandings and future clarity—not just for themselves, but for a larger evolutionary process.

If Judas carried an immense, unresolved charge of divine participation that was mistaken for betrayal, that energy may now seek resolution through those capable of holding both the depth of his role and the love required to restore it. If his story has been distorted over time, then those who are drawn to it in a transformative way may be helping to shift his narrative within the collective consciousness.

When my journey with Judas began, I considered the possibility of being his reincarnation. My connection to him felt profound, tangible, and I related to him with an intensity that was difficult to explain. However, I do not believe I am Judas reincarnated, yet hold the possibility of holding a fragment of him. Even before researching various traditions, I instinctively used the term "fragment" to describe my experience. As my journey unfolded, this theme of fragmentation continued to arise in my visions and reflections.

My connection to Judas remains mysterious—perhaps one day it will be fully understood. In the meantime, I resonate with those who ponder the role of carrying an aspect, fragment, or spark of another being and hope to fulfill whatever responsibilities may come with it.

While I may never fully comprehend the complexities of my experience, I am content to live within the mystery. I remain open to perspectives that seek to explain the extraordinary, yet I find comfort in holding the unknown as sacred. There are aspects of existence that transcend concrete understanding, and I embrace the beauty of that mystery.

Truth

My beloved partner, Krishna, had a dream one night. A figure, as black as night, came to the sliding glass door in our bedroom. Krishna got up and opened the door for this presence. She told Krishna that she was not here to see him but to see me. She mentioned to Krishna that in order for me to have the strength to navigate the darkness, I had to answer three questions:

>What am I most afraid of?
>What am I attached to?
>What am I willing to live for?

Reflecting upon the dream, I felt a connection between the message Krishna received and my experience with Judas. I felt the dark figure not as malevolent but as a presence like the Black Madonna or the Dark Mother, a divine being of creation and destruction, a warrior of light in the darkness. The 'darkness' I needed the strength to navigate through was not necessarily about evil but about realities intentionally concealed, truths that had been hidden, and distortion. The 'darkness' was also the darkness that brings forth creation: a dark womb that fosters the development of life; the darkness of a planted seed that allows for germination; and even the inner shadow work that brings liberation and the creation of a new, restored self.

I thought about the questions for a few weeks, and several answers arose that felt superficial. One day in a sweat lodge, all the questions were answered with the same response: *the truth.*

> I am afraid of speaking the truth.
> I am most attached to knowing the truth.
> I am willing to live for the truth.

I was amazed that the three questions had the same answer as I was expecting three unique responses. I was also surprised that the thing I was most attached to was something positive: *the truth.* I assumed that the answer to the second question would be linked to something I was afraid to let go of or something my ego was attached to that was not in my highest good. I acknowledged the cultural conditioning of thought that I fell into, specifically a negative connotation of being attached to anything. This whole experience with Judas has encouraged me to go beyond cultural programming, so I was not surprised to see the conditioning of my thoughts being brought to light while attempting to answer the three questions.

Being attached to truth made me realize that being attached to something is not always limiting but can lead to motivation, determination, and bravery. The attachment to truth leads to a positive and invigorating experience as it fosters strength and focus. It is an attachment that brings steadfastness, a courage to speak, a strength in navigating a difficult path, and the endurance to keep reaching for the highest truth I can access. Being attached to knowing the truth means holding a tight grip, not letting go, and not giving up on my purpose and commitment to Judas, regardless.

Though I do not claim to have accessed Judas's ultimate truth, merely speaking my truth about my journeys and what unfolded can be daunting at times. When I look at the fears of speaking my truth, such as facing the cruelty from others who violently contest those who present views contrary to conventional thought, the fears dissipate and lose their power. Being *attached* to the truth empowers me to face those who wish to *attack* opposing views viciously. Being willing to live for the truth, as well as being attached to the truth, are both empowering me not only to write this book but also to publish it.

I can sense that under the fear of speaking my truth is an actual fear of the truth itself. I imagine the truth being so big that it would not only deconstruct me, all notions of self, but also perhaps my entire existence. Because of my attachment to truth, I am willing to not only live for this truth but also to deconstruct / die to this truth. Not die physically, but a death of self, if need be.

The ironic thing is that I am willing to live for the ultimate truth of Judas, but I don't know if that is obtainable while I am alive. The ultimate truth may only be accessible after my physical death, where my soul might have access to Judas's infinite wisdom. It is quite a paradox to be willing to live for something that might not be obtainable to me while alive in my physical form.

It is liberating not to be attached to needing to be right but being attached to a deep longing to personally experience truth: the eternal, absolute, and perfect knowledge of all that is. I suppose we can only grasp a mere fraction of the ultimate, Divine truth while still in form. I do not claim truth in this book or elsewhere; instead, I offer a sincere and heart-based exploration in pursuit of truth related to the mystery of Judas. This book is my attempt to express a perspective of Judas that relates to the mysteries of the heavens and our existence.

The Structure of This Book

Five years ago, as I sat next to my bed, I looked over at my fleece bedspread and saw an outline of a hand holding a book imprinted into the purple fabric. I was deeply amazed and bewildered. I felt it was meaningful, yet I had no idea what the significance was nor how that happened. When Spirit asked if I would write about Judas, my memory flashed back to that moment, and I finally understood that the imprint of the hand holding a book was related to this very publication.

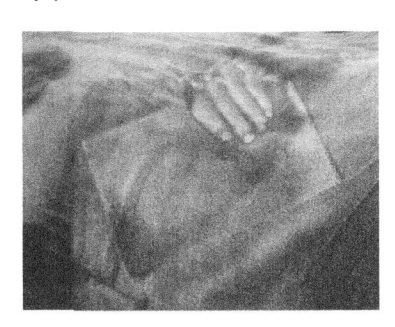

This book came together into five parts. After this introduction, in Part 2, I share my journeys with Judas and offer some initial reflections and contemplations about the visions. In Part 3, I share my deeper pondering about the mysteries of Judas as well as the power of myth, notions of martyrdom and sacrifice, and contemplations of Judas as the "13th God." Part 4 explores Judas as an "authentic facilitator" who mirrors humanity's deepest shadows and unconscious betrayals, drawing on Michael Brown's insights from *The Chameleon Mirror*. In the last section, Part 5, I share how carrying a fragment / aspect / spark of Judas may have shaped some of my life experiences.

As you journey through this manuscript, please be aware that the terms God, Creator, Great Spirit, and Almighty Loving Presence are used interchangeably.

Part 2: Journeying with Judas

A Random Thought

One sunny day back in 2013, a random thought crossed my mind as I was going for a walk, "*I think we have the story of Judas wrong. He was not a betrayer.*" It was an out of the blue thought. I didn't ponder it much, nor did I wonder if the story isn't correct, what is the accurate historical account? What significance would it hold if Judas was not a betrayer? If he wasn't a betrayer, who was he?

Everything I learned as a child attending a Catholic grade school asserted that Judas committed an evil deed; he was the traitor who handed over beloved Jesus for blood money. By doing such an act, it was through extension that Judas betrayed God himself. Judas was more than an immoral biblical figure; he was the ultimate archetype of treachery and betrayal. Yet, in this brief moment, this construct of Judas did not resonate with me at all. It is significant to me that out of all the random thoughts that have crossed my mind in my decades of life, that I even remember this pondering as it wasn't extensive, and if I remember correctly, my thoughts about Judas didn't last more than a minute or two. I didn't even stop to consider why on Earth I was even thinking about Judas.

From Hell to the House of the Lord

Two years later, in the spring of 2015, Judas reappeared. Yet, this time not as a fleeting thought but in an intense dream:

I was attending an event of a clairvoyant individual who was about to give a psychic reading for all the attendees. I walked into the event from the back of the room. As I walked down the middle aisle looking for a seat, the reader recognized me as Judas. This recognition was mysterious because I was in the form of myself as Kerry. It was as if he witnessed my inner essence, my soul, as Judas's.

Upon identifying me as Judas, the clairvoyant reader became increasingly upset with me to the point of becoming livid. He started to yell at me, accusing me of betraying Jesus. In response to him, I became energetically huge. My physical frame did not expand, but my energy increased into an enormous force. I spoke firmly and loudly to him.

I spoke as Judas and said, "At the time, I died for Jesus. I love myself for this. I honor myself for this. I thank myself for this. At the time, I died for Jesus, but now I choose to live. I choose to love and to flourish and be profoundly alive. I choose to no longer live in the depths of hell. I choose to live in Christ's love, within the loving embrace of the Lord. I choose to live, not on the outskirts of the embrace, but in the embrace. While in the embrace, I choose to actively receive all the grace and love that is being poured out to me in this moment. I shall live in the house of the Lord forever!!"

Contemplations:

I woke with a strange mixture of feeling the dream was out of the ordinary and at the same time somehow natural and even expected. Judas choosing to be loved and to live in the embrace of the Lord was not only comprehensible but felt appropriate and even wonderful. The details of the dream didn't faze me; however, I wondered about my connection to Judas and if his essence / consciousness had entered my dream space.

When Judas spoke through my physical vessel, I felt like I was him. Since I could not sense the difference between us in the dream, and because the psychic reader recognized me as Judas, I wondered about the possibility of being the reincarnation of Judas. At the time, I did not know about the notion of fragments, sparks, or aspects, as I mentioned in this book's introduction. For me, it was more of an all or nothing experience; either one is or is not the reincarnation of a being. I wasn't disturbed by the possibility of being the reincarnation of Judas, regardless of what has been said about him for nearly 2000 years. Genuinely, I would not have minded being Judas as there was no feeling of him being evil nor a betrayer. In fact, I felt an unexplainable connection to him as well as a tender love.

The amount of energy I felt upon waking was enormous. I felt so enlivened. In the dream, Judas's lifeforce felt unstoppable and impenetrable, and that energy followed me into the waking state. Judas felt like a force to be reckoned with that had zero wiggle room for any nonsense. Judas had zero tolerance for being called a betrayer and being accused of anything that was not true. As Judas spoke, it felt like he was shattering false structures and dismantling the rubbish that came from the fabrications.

In the dream, Judas stood up to the reader, claimed his truth, and declared he was no longer living in the depths of hell but in the house of the Lord. This declaration speaks to an understanding of salvation—not as an external redemption granted by another, but as a self-initiated return to divine love. Salvation, in this dream, felt like Judas reclaiming his rightful place in the greater design of existence. His choice to live fully in divine embrace felt like a message that salvation was not bestowed upon the worthy but rather claimed by anyone who comes to recognize their inherent belonging.

Cutting the Unbiblical Cord

A few months after this dream, I had a past-life regression. I had been speaking with a regression specialist about a childhood experience that I could not understand. I explained to her that when I was growing up, I sensed an invisible noose hanging in the family room. It was invisible, but it was very real to me. It was so present that I would never walk in that space and always walked around the noose as if it was physically present. As a child, I never mentioned this to anyone. In my adult life, it remained a mystery. The specialist suggested a regression to see what information might be available.

The regression unfolded as follows:

I went to the time of Jesus. The ground was pale yellow and rocky. It was breezy and a little cold outside. I was a barefoot girl around 14 years old, wearing a long, dark blue dress made out of heavy fabric. I was petite.

As the regression started, I was alone and rushing home. I was worried because I knew someone was dying. As I entered the house, it was Joseph, the husband of Mary, who was dying. When I saw him, he called me "dear one," and I could feel the love, tenderness, and yet frailty in his voice. Mary and I knelt on either side of Joseph.

The regression specialist asked if there was anyone else in the room. I looked around and noticed Archangel Michael. Archangel Michael placed his hand on my heart and said, "You are far greater than you allow yourself to be." He told me he was there to assist me in being 'far greater' and to help me 'claim my dignity.'

The regression specialist guided me to ask Archangel Michael about the noose. I asked and then listened for a response. He said the noose was "not linked to anything valid." Archangel Michael went onto explain that the noose symbolized being bound by human perspectives and its many variations. If it was linked to anything, it was to sickness, stuck-ness, and stories, but not connected to divine perfection, freedom, and truth. He encouraged me to be sovereign and to break free of any agreements that kept me in thoughts, emotions, and perspectives that were not true. He said that I accepted many falsities in my life, and I did not need to agree any longer. Archangel Michael also said that the noose not being linked to anything valid also symbolized there being nothing to atone.

Then the regression shifted, and I was then in my early twenties. I was in a field, and off in the distance, I could see Judas dead, and I wept and wept upon this sight. My hands curled into fists, and I sobbed, not in my mind's eye, but during the regression. In my mind's eye, I saw a vision of myself screaming with so much pain. I was so distraught and filled with rage and agony as I believed Judas didn't have to die for what he did. I understood his mission. I would have stopped his death if I could have.

The regression specialist guided me to call Judas's soul to me and "channel God's love to him." As I called upon his soul, he was strikingly present and very loving. Judas was much taller than me as I only came up to the area of his heart. Judas had broad shoulders and was strong, mighty, and appeared as a powerful angelic being. A knowing emerged that though we had been separated at the time of death on Earth, I had never let go of Judas. I also knew that somehow my love for Judas had been restoring him over time.

As the regression progressed, I was in heaven with Judas and Jesus. Jesus was holding space for us and being a loving witness. Judas was beautiful and kind. He held me to his chest, and as he looked at me, his eyes poured with love for me. He loved me so much that I started to weep. Again, I cried during the regression, not in the visions of my mind's eye.

Judas gently removed the noose from my neck, untied the knot, and draped the rope over his right arm. After he untied it, the noose was just a rope with no power in it. All energy that was bound in the knot was released. He dropped the rope from heaven to the Earth, where it dissolved.

As I attempted to communicate to the regression specialist about what was going on, I tried to tell her the rope was my umbilical cord that plugged me into a matrix. Yet, the word unbiblical came out instead of umbilical. Judas guided me to unplug from the illusions of matrix, reconnect with my soul and Jesus, as well as open myself to love, gratitude, and joy, and the deep knowing of my own worthiness.

Judas then poured an enormous amount of water onto me. It was so much water it made me laugh out loud. The water fell to Earth from heaven. He looked at me and said, "You are a precious dear child. Your burden has been great." Then Judas turned to a grayish stone, crumbled into ash, and returned to Earth. The rope, the water, and the ash had fallen from heaven to Earth, joining the two realms. It was also an act of clearing a false story (embedded in the noose) and the pain and anguish that came with this false story.

I remained in the heavenly space with Jesus. Jesus said, "Please come." He held me and comforted me like one would a child. He shared, "I am here for you, precious one. I love you so much." Jesus mentioned the Biblical story is incorrect and that Judas has become a part of a cultural structure, yet these structures are crumbling. Jesus shared that there is a truth beyond what people think or understand. All unfolded divinely. Jesus said, "Do not consider Judas as Divine. Know him as Divine."

As we neared the end of the regression, the practitioner asked if there was any information that I needed to know. In being silent and waiting, a correlation between Judas and Mary Magdalene became evident as they were both wrongly labeled. Mary was marked as a prostitute, and Judas was labeled as a traitor. Both were labeled to suppress a truth.

At the very end of the regression, there was an angel present as well as a young child. When the regression specialist asked who the child was, she felt like my own.

<u>Contemplations</u>:

Upon coming out of the regression, I debriefed with the practitioner. I shared with her that I felt like I was a "soul fragment of Judas." It was like who I am, what makes up my essence, was an aspect of Judas. It wasn't merely that I had a fragment that belonged to him. It felt like this fragment made up my essence: "I am" a soul fragment of Judas. There was no mention or vision of being a fragment in the session; it was a feeling that I was left with upon completion of the regression. I had no idea what it would mean to be a soul fragment or have a soul fragment of Judas or anyone else. This regression experience enhanced my curiosity about my connection with Judas, the curiosity that was sparked by my initial dream.

What was profoundly interesting to me was the raw emotion that I felt during the regression. When I started to cry in the session, it was like my chest was cracking open. This was no shallow cry. I wondered where such deep emotion came from and why did I feel so strongly about Judas. The love and tenderness I felt led to me wonder if I had been Judas's wife and the child was ours. The knowing that emerged that I had never let go of him, even after his death, and somehow my love for him had been restoring him over time felt so familiar and yet unexplainable.

The notion of connecting heaven and Earth returned in future visions. What does it mean to join heaven and Earth? Are they not already connected? Is there a separation between the two realms? What would it mean that a noose (holding a false story), cleansing water, and Judas himself in the form of ash could link heaven and Earth? Was there divine information that was reaching the Earth through the work of Judas? Was he doing anything at all? When we enter into other realms of consciousness, are we doing something or just having visions?

I wonder if Archangel Michael stating that the noose was not linked to anything valid and to break free of stories that are not true, related to Judas's death. I did not come out of this regression with an understanding that Judas did not hang himself. It was only in listening to the recording of the regression years later that the possible connection dawned on me. Perhaps there was so much religious programming during my youth that this information was not able to penetrate. At that time, I understood the noose being removed from my neck as healing for me. It took future dreams for information about Judas not hanging himself but being killed to be considered as a real possibility.

Banished to Hell as Judas

In January 2016, I had a vivid and intense dream.

In this dream, I was Judas. As the dream started, I was lying on the bare dirt in an open grave. The grave was a rather large square, not narrow like one made for a coffin. I was not buried very deeply. I was lying in the grave, dammed to hell as Judas. It was nighttime, and all was dark. I could make out the silhouettes and some faces of people above me. They were angry and throwing stones on top of me.

I wasn't bothered by any of this. I felt no physical or emotional pain, I wasn't worried, and I was strangely calm for such a situation. I knew I was Judas, and I knew I was damned to hell, and the damning came from these people, not from God. I wondered what to do to get out of hell. I called upon assistance from Spirit. I asked in a sing-song kind of manner, "So, I seem to have found myself damned to hell. I am just wondering if there happens to be any rituals to reverse damnation. If so, do you think you can help me?"

As soon as I asked, the experience started to shift. The people went away, the rocks dissolved, and the grave rose to the Earth's surface. I was no longer buried. In fact, I no longer had a body. I was an unbounded presence.

It was then daylight. I was no longer at the gravesite but could see it off in the distance. The site was a large, beautiful meadow with a small, rounded hill. All was bright, and it was a beautiful day. Time seemed to be going by quickly as I could see flowers in the process of growing and blooming.

<u>Contemplations</u>:

In this dream, I had no awareness of myself as Kerry. I *was* Judas, embodied in his broad male form. Since it felt very natural to be Judas in the dream state, I awoke with a mixture of feelings and questions. Why did it feel so natural to be him? Is there a possibility that I could be Judas? On the one hand, it felt natural to be Judas in the dream, and on the other hand, I was perplexed.

This dream happened in January of 2016. Three years later, in January of 2019, I found out that the *Gospel of Judas* had been discovered in the late 1970s in Egypt and published in 2006 by National Geographic. In the *Gospel of Judas*, it states that Judas knew that if he carried out the task of handing over Jesus, as Jesus asked him to, that the other disciples would hate him, curse him, and stone him to death. At the time of this dream, the possibility that Judas knew he would be stoned to death and cursed by generations to come was not in my awareness.

There was information about Judas's death in this dream as I saw people throwing stones on top of me. Yet, similar to my past-life regression, this understanding did not register. It is amazing how information can be present but not received. If Spirit or Judas's essence was trying to communicate with me about how Judas died, the information did not register. It wasn't until a journey in 2018, where I saw Judas being stoned to death, that I received the communication very clearly. As stated in the introduction, I do not claim to know Judas's ultimate truth; I can only ponder what was revealed to me and why.

This dream stirred many questions: what does it mean to be damned to hell, let alone break free; what does it mean to be cursed and to reverse a curse; what does all this mean for Judas as well as for humanity?

To me, hell is not a place but a level of consciousness that we can experience during our lives as well as after our physical deaths. The difference between heaven and hell can be how close or how far we feel from God as well as our souls. The phrase, *'a living hell,'* captures the excruciating pain we can endure while we are alive. This living hell is not a place but a state of deep inner chaos, agony, anguish, misery, and fragmentation. It may be possible that this same state of consciousness continues after death, especially if one carries unresolved suffering.

If we are in a state of a living hell when we are alive, our souls might take that experience into our afterlife. In my work, I have assisted some souls after they died. One person was a young woman who had committed suicide and was disoriented after her passing. Another was a man who had struggled with alcoholism and was not fully aware that he had passed. It was explained to me that if someone is very addicted to a substance, there is a possibility that their souls can look for that substance after they pass. For this particular man, it seemed like he was still looking for a beer. It makes me wonder about what realm or level of consciousness he was stuck in. Are such realms hellish experiences for the soul?

I do not believe God casts souls into hell. But I do believe that people—and non-benevolent forces—can attempt to trap others in such states, both in life and after death. Energetically speaking, damning someone to hell is the opposite of praying for them. The positive effects of a group of people praying for an individual or even a community have been witnessed, experienced, and even scientifically studied. If prayer can uplift a soul, what is the power of collective condemnation? Shamanic traditions speak of *psychic daggers*—when a person sends hatred toward another, that energy crystallizes in the recipient's auric field, affecting their mind, emotions, and even physical well-being. If even one person's rage can cause such harm, what destruction happens when a furious collective turns its condemnation onto a single soul?

The concept of hell or an equivalent state of suffering varies widely across religious and mystical traditions. Some traditions see it as a literal place of eternal punishment, while others view it as a state of consciousness, a temporary realm of purification, or an illusion created by the mind.

Traditional Christian teachings, especially in Catholic and Protestant theology, have long depicted hell as a place of *eternal damnation* reserved for those who reject God. However, alternative Christian perspectives challenge this portrayal. The Eastern Orthodox Church does not view hell as a physical place but as *a state of separation from God*. Mystical Christian thinkers have argued that hell is not a punishment inflicted by God, but a state created by one's own refusal to accept divine love.

Judaism does not traditionally have a concept of eternal damnation. Early texts describe the afterlife as Sheol, a shadowy realm of unconscious existence for all souls. Later, Gehinnom emerged as a place of temporary purification, where even the gravest sinners undergo soul-cleansing for up to 12 months before moving on. Jewish mysticism (Kabbalah) introduces *Tikkun HaNefesh* (soul correction), emphasizing that fragmented or wounded souls can be healed over time.

Islamic teachings describe Jahannam as a realm of purification or punishment, where souls may be temporarily or permanently placed based on their actions and intentions. In Hindu thought, there is no eternal damnation, but souls can experience Naraka, a temporary realm of suffering based on karmic consequences. Naraka is *not permanent*—it serves as a purging process before reincarnation.

Theosophy, a mystical philosophy blending Eastern and Western esotericism, does not see hell as a literal place but rather as an astral plane of consciousness. A soul that dies in distress, regret, or guilt may become stuck in Kāmaloka, the lower astral realm, until it resolves its attachments. Theosophy teaches that no soul remains trapped forever; through the release of karmic burdens, all beings eventually move toward spiritual evolution.

Many Indigenous traditions do not have a fixed "hell" but speak of spiritual imbalance that can cause suffering after death. Some traditions (e.g., certain Native American and Siberian beliefs) describe lost souls who cannot transition to the afterlife due to unresolved trauma.

Gnostic Christianity holds a radical view: the real hell is physical existence itself. Gnostics believed the material world was a prison created by the Demiurge, a false god, and that Jesus came to reveal the path of liberation.

If Judas was killed by people full of fury and rage, what energetically happened to Judas at his death? Did their collective hatred cast a spell of damnation upon him? What influence did they hold over Judas's soul? Did the way Judas die cause his soul to fragment? What is the significance of Judas's death and afterlife? What difference does it make for Christianity if Judas was killed or if he committed suicide? What is the significance if his soul went to heaven or the consciousness of hell?

If my experiences align with mystical perspectives, I may not have been helping Judas as an individual *in hell* but rather participating in the *spiritual redemption of his name*.

The Dawn That is Awakening

Five months later, in May 2016, I received a message that did not involve Judas but felt significant within the context of my journey with him.

I had what felt to be a very long and endless night of rest. I kept opening my eyes and thinking that the sun must be rising soon. Time would pass, and all I could think was, "The sun must be rising by now." I kept opening my eyes expecting to see the light of day. Finally, I settled into my heart, resisting the temptation to see the light, and realized I was missing a message from Spirit: "The Son has risen. The Sun has risen in you. The Christ Consciousness is the dawn you are expecting to see with your eyes. It is the dawn that is awakening in your heart."

Contemplations:

At the time of this experience, I had not thought about this message within the context of my journey with Judas. Yet, while reflecting, I wondered if this too was a piece of the mystery that was unfolding. What was truly awakening in my heart? What inward shifts needed to happen in order for me to step into my role as it relates to Judas?

Motherly Love

My connection to Judas quieted down for two and a half years, and then in the autumn of 2018, I had multiple dreams and journeys, some of which remain beyond comprehension, and their explanation is still a puzzlement. Below are the details of the visions I had, along with some contemplations.

I could see Judas approaching me from a short distance away. I was not surprised. Seeing him was not strange to me as it felt as natural as seeing a long-lost relative who I was expecting to see. When Judas arrived, I embraced him with motherly love. The maternal love felt tender, as well as fierce and protective. Experiencing the deep love for Judas was as natural as breathing air, and his presence felt appropriate, expected, and greatly welcomed.

<u>Contemplations</u>:

At the time of this journey, it had been two and a half years since I had the dream of Judas being damned to hell. I woke feeling how lovely it was to see him and that it felt too long since I had. The motherly love I felt for Judas reminded me of my past-life regression, where I experienced such deep emotion for Judas. Feeling the love as a motherly love felt so beautiful and natural, yet still unexplainable as to why such sincere and deep sentiments would be present.

Embedded in the Truth is a Power

This journey began with a clear message from Spirit: I was not to hand over my power to the authorities. In this case, the authorities were the religious leaders. This power included my truth as well as the truth of Judas. The suppression of the truth was associated with a corresponding suppression of power. This truth was a begotten truth.

As the journey continued, I felt Spirit asking me to receive and trust; to be present to new knowledge; to be uncompromisingly open, and to allow and let be.

<u>Contemplations</u>:

A 'begotten' truth to me is a truth born from God, not made by humans or false gods. Spirit mentioned that embedded in the truth was a distinct power, and I wondered what the truth was specifically and what tremendous power was rooted in it. I feel that no one holds the ultimate truth of Judas, other than God and Judas himself. Thus, I question what am I holding? How much of what I envisioned and experienced was accurate? How much can I not even begin to fathom, and what is yet to be revealed? I wonder what I can do to support Judas in anchoring in his truth to the planet and, at the same time, question if he even needs my support.

I can understand why this message from Spirit, not to hand over my power, came before more was revealed about Judas in my journeys to follow. What was about to unfold was well beyond the common understanding of Judas. Owning the truth of my experience with Judas was an undertaking unto itself. The notion of having an aspect, fragment, or spark of another being is not commonly understood. Those that understand have their personal adventures to share. Some who don't understand or even believe it is possible have tried to reframe my experience to fit their understandings of how the world works. Staying true to my knowing that this is not mere archetypal work, that there is a much bigger mystery to be explored, has been important to me.

Reflecting upon the three questions from Krishna's dream *(what am I most afraid of, what am I attached to, and what am I willing to live for?)*, I acknowledge one of my biggest fears is speaking the truth. Though I do not claim the ultimate truth in this book, I am offering my journeys that provide a very different perspective, and that alone is daunting to present. Handing over my power could be as simple as disregarding my journeys because others do not understand them or because they contradict traditional knowledge. The desire to live for the truth and being attached to the truth provides me with the strength to share.

Over the years, I have been building the strength and capacity of claiming my truth and my power. Part of my journey has been recognizing what it means to hand over my power and in what circumstances that occurs. It has also been about exploring what it means to be in my power, not as a vague concept but as an experience. Though these lessons have been personal to me, I feel we are existing in a time where we, as a collective, have been reclaiming our power and our truth; a time of questioning authority and structures; a time where we are vehemently shining a light on the falsities to which we once adhered.

I felt Spirit asking me to receive, honor, trust, and be present to new knowledge as well as an unthinkable perspective on Judas; to allow information to come through without judgment or attachment. I felt that being present was not just listening but being unboundedly present ('unbounded' from old teachings) and experiencing from the level of my soul (not from my conditioned mind).

The Bedroom Tomb

I was with Jesus in my childhood room. I was an adult in this journey, not my child self. My room seemed much smaller than I remembered it to be. It also felt heavy, encumbered by furniture, and with a density in the air.

Jesus referred to my childhood room as a tomb and said that a tomb was no place for life. Jesus asked, "Why are you here when there has been a resurrection?" Jesus was referring to a resurrection within myself that I had not acknowledged. The part of me that had not accepted the resurrection was stuck in the past and still in the tomb. Jesus said this aspect of my childhood was no longer happening, yet I lived as if this was still occurring.

To help me heal this stuck aspect of myself, Jesus pulled fragments of me into my being and collapsed all ages of me into the present moment. By doing so, he helped me heal and integrate an aspect of my childhood trauma that I had been living with, and that was continuing to impact my adult life. Jesus stated, "Move on. You need to move on in order to do the work you are here to do." We exited the tomb of my bedroom.

Contemplations:

It seemed significant that I was my adult-self in this journey, not my child-self. I wonder, for me to do what I am here to do, if part of me cannot be stuck in childhood. Perhaps I need a certain amount of maturity to navigate my experiences with Judas and 'resurrect' any information related to Judas that is calling to be awakened. The room feeling heavy made it feel more like a tomb than a bedroom. The bulky furniture reminded me of structures, both material and cultural, that can burden and inhibit our lives. It was beautiful to exit the tomb of my bedroom at the end of this journey.

Jesus asking, "Why are you here when there has been a resurrection" reminded me of a bible verse where Jesus asked Mary, "Why do you look for the living among the dead? He is not here; he has risen!" (Luke 24: 5-6). I can see how my former upbringing in the church shaped my dream space. In my journey, Jesus referred to a resurrection within myself that I had not acknowledged nor fully anchored into my being. I reflected on my experience in May 2016 when I received the message: *The Son has risen. The Sun has risen in you. The Christ Consciousness is the dawn you are expecting to see with your eyes. It is the dawn that is awakening in your heart.* The sense of awakening in my heart felt similar to what Jesus referred to as an inner resurrection.

Though I did not receive specific information about what part of me was still living in the past, I completely understood how my childhood experience has impacted my adult life over the years. When I was experiencing the timelines collapsing, there was an expansiveness that arose as well as an intersection of child and adult, innocence and wisdom, and so forth. This sense of all-inclusiveness that leads to a sense of boundlessness returns in future journeys.

Roc-a-Sha

I was standing outside of a tomb. A large tombstone that, in height, was well above my head was present. I was holding a rock that had been cut out from the tombstone. The rock was a sizable stone, a bit bigger than a basketball. It was significant that the rock came from the tombstone and was not a random rock from the ground.

I was standing next to the large tombstone when I heard Spirit call me by the name, Roc-a-Sha. Roc-a-Sha meant rock cut from the tombstone. The tombstone was related to Jesus. The rock, which was cut from the tombstone, was related to Judas. Though the name Roc-a-Sha in its totality meant rock cut from the tombstone, the individual parts had their meaning:

Roc = referred to the rock, Judas
a = a universal reunion
Sha = refereed to The Comforter, Jesus.

As the journey continued, I sensed Judas behind me and saw Jesus in front of me. We were all in the form of our spirits, not in our physical bodies. The three of us then merged into one.

Contemplations:

Combining the messages from the last journey and this one, I had been taken out of my tomb and given a name. It was like I was going through a birth process.

I have heard Jesus referred to as the rock, but in this case, Jesus was the Comforter, and the consciousness of resurrection symbolized as the tombstone. Judas being the rock was profoundly fascinating to me as it was such a different construct than the one I learned as a child. I wondered if Judas was the new rock, the new foundation? If so, what foundation would that be?

There is a saying, 'cut from the same cloth.' In this journey, Judas was 'cut from the same rock,' so to speak. The rock was specific to the tombstone and, therefore, the *story* of Jesus's resurrection. Was this symbolizing the rebirth of Judas? If Judas was 'cut from the same rock' as Jesus, does Judas carry a profound power / significance / role that has been overlooked or not understood?

Stigmata

I was lying down resting when Spirit called me to an altar. I did not want to go as I knew I was being asked to receive the stigmata. I wondered why on earth would I receive the stigmata when I didn't feel that close to Jesus. Why would Spirit ask something as serious as receiving stigmata?

Spirit continued to call, and a desire arose to respond to the invitation. I built up the courage to walk to the altar. I saw other people close to the altar, but most of them were asleep and not paying any attention to me. That was good as I did not want people to see me if I decided to go through with this request.

I am not sure what shifted in me as I approached the altar. I went from thinking that this does not make any sense to being willing. There was a shift in my thinking without a corresponding process. Somehow when I got to the altar, I was ready and no longer had the question of why.

I stood at the altar and told Spirit what I would agree to, and what I would not. Something had shifted in my willingness, but I had terms and conditions. I firmly stated, "I agree to receive the stigmata. I will not endure any physical pain. The markings are not to be seen by anyone. This is the only way I will do this."

I received the stigmata energetically, without blood or markings. As energetic imprints from Jesus, the stigmata were beautiful geometric patterns of light that hovered over my palms, feet, and side and then merged with me. It was a magical and wondrous experience.

<u>Contemplations</u>:

Linking the journeys together, I had been taken out of a tomb, given a name, and imprinted with the stigmata. What was unfolding? Was this part of an ongoing initiation to prepare me for my work with Judas, to help me gain the strength to navigate and share the unconventional and unexplainable experiences with Judas that were yet to come? Was this a ritual to establish an appropriate vibrational foundation for my work as Roc-a-Sha?

The geometric patterns and the energy they contained felt so pure and beautiful, yet what exactly was embedded in the stigmata and what was the purpose? Though I felt safe, guided, and loved, I did not fully understand what all this meant for Judas or me. What was happening to me, through me, and as me as Roc-a-Sha?

The Egg of Earth and Heaven

I was at the base of a beautiful staircase that led to heaven. The staircase was made of light and spiraled upward. Since I was deeply afraid of heaven and even more terrified to go, I didn't dare to journey up the steps. I had two distinct thoughts:

1. *If I go, I will be asked to take on responsibilities outside of my comfort zone. I like being meek, quiet, and reserved. Going to heaven explodes my comfort zone and my desire to be introverted.*

2. *Going to heaven and doing what God asks means some type of punishment will be bestowed upon me as there is a link between great heavenly assignments and punishment, even though the punishment is not from God but people.*

The feeling was complex. If I go to heaven, I will be asked to do great things. Somehow doing great things leads to emotional pain as well as punishment.

As the journey continued, an energetic help 'button' was installed above my heart, in the upper left side of my chest just beneath my collar bone. It was not a physical button, but an energetic button made of light, similar to the stigmata. If I was ever afraid of heaven or afraid in general, I could touch this spot, and help would appear. I was encouraged to touch the button, and as I did, an egg was formed around me. The earth came up from below, and the heavens came down from above, which left me encased in a protective egg. In this egg, made of heaven and earth, I was safe. In this egg, the association of great heavenly assignments with punishment was being dissolved.

<u>Contemplations</u>:

Along with being taken out of a tomb, given a name and the stigmata, I received an energetic help button, for which I was extremely grateful. The help button was not only to soothe the rising fear but also to provide healing of what caused the fear. When the egg formed around me, I felt the association of great heavenly assignments with punishment being dissolved.

The egg of earth and heaven felt like a symbol of integration. Deep healing happens not by ascending away from earthly experience, nor by being swallowed by it, but by holding both heaven and earth within us. The alchemy of uniting seemingly opposing forces—spiritual and material, light and dark, judgment and grace—aligns with the idea that true transformation is not about escaping one realm for another but about integrating all aspects into wholeness.

From Judas's perspective, I can understand the association between being asked to take on a great responsibility with punishment for the completion of the task. Though I can understand this journey from Judas's perspective, why have I felt similar feelings in my own life; why would I have this similarity with Judas?

I wondered what it meant to have an aspect or a fragment of someone else. If Judas did fragment, did each element carry specific energy? Was I carrying the fragment that contained the energies of damnation, hatred from others, and being ostracized?

I was beginning to wonder if my entanglement with Judas impacted some of my life experiences, such as being ostracized as a child and feeling like I have done something so wrong God cannot love me. I dive into this connection more in Part 5 of this book, but this was when I started to wonder about the notion of carrying a fragment of someone else and if that fragment then imprints the life of the carrier.

As my mind pondered about our connection, I was mentally entertained by Judas's last name, Iscariot. When said slowly, Iscariot sounds like is-Keri-ot. Keri is my name, simply spelled differently. The suffix ot is used to form a masculine noun from a feminine noun. With the suffix present, it is a male noun with the root being the female. Judas Iscariot; Judas Is-Keri-ot. I am not implying that his name has anything to do with me or that my name has anything to do with Kerioth. My mind was simply playing and rather entertained as I pondered how intertwined I felt with Judas.

Religious scholars have speculated where Judas's last name originated. Some biblical historians believe that Iscariot is derived from the Latin word sicarius, meaning murderer. In contrast, others think Judas's surname links him to the Sicarii, a Jewish group who were a part of the radical movement of zealots. Though there is no definite conclusion, a common explanation is that Iscariot might be a combination of the Hebrew words ish, and Kerioth indicating that Judas was a man who came from a place called Kerioth. There are two locations called Kerioth mentioned in the bible, one in the southern part of Israel (Joshua 15:25) and the other in the country of Moab, outside of Israel (Jeremiah 48:24, 41). Scholars cannot confirm that Judas was from either place (Ehrman, 2006, p. 145-146). It is fascinating that we don't have conclusive evidence of what his name means, yet so much meaning has been given to him and his name. Who is Judas? What do we truly know about him?

Altered at the Altar

In this journey, I could not distinguish between Judas and myself. There was such an overlap of myself with Judas that I felt like two people in one. Jesus asked the question, "Who are you when you believe you have done something wrong?" I responded, "I am mournful, apologetic, and sometimes so hard on myself, I can barely function. It is like I beat up and destroy myself for making a mistake. I fear that others will hurt me if I make a mistake, and therefore I take care of the flogging before they do. I self-destruct before others destroy me."

Jesus asked, "Are you destroying yourself with someone else's belief that you have done something wrong? Or is it your knowing you have made a mistake?" I responded, "I take their belief, or what I assume they are believing, and

I turn their belief into a self-flogging mechanism. I keep myself in a perpetual hell with the energy of others."

Jesus encouraged me to stand in honor, to admit to only what I have truly done wrong and no more, and not to commit myself to the hell of shame and guilt that is summoned by other's untrue beliefs. Jesus made the distinction between the truth of responsibility and the falsity of responsibility; taking ownership of what one has done versus taking ownership of what one has not done. Jesus encouraged me to stand in my honor and my integrity. From that place, assume full responsibility for my behavior and discard the responsibility others have wrongfully assigned to me. Jesus encouraged me to love myself and forgive myself. I was to forgive myself for forgetting myself. I was to forgive the forgetting.

I began to understand the difference between being destroyed and being altered. Being destroyed by my mistakes was likened to self-destruction and beating myself up. This process did not result in self-forgiveness and transformation; it only led to self-loathing and self-punishment—a perpetual hell. Being altered by my mistakes contained death and rebirth. This death was not self-destruction linked to punishment. It was the destruction that the Phoenix knows, the destruction that brings birth and transformation without self-harm. This destruction was aligned with being altered and altered for the specific purpose of ascension (meaning ascending beyond my old self). The Phoenix knows the exact time this is to be done.

I was told by Spirit that I need an altar to do this kind of sacred alteration. This altar does not need to be a physical structure with candles and crystals; it can be in my heart.

At this altar, there was to be no magic wand as not everything was meant to be healed in a flash. Healing was not about getting through the pain but about gaining wisdom from experiences. The magic of not having a magic wand and having things heal and disappear in a flash was that we could experience the nature of what we were enduring as it dissipated. There was medicine and wisdom that could be missed in pain and discomfort disappearing in a flash.

<u>Contemplations:</u>

I wonder if Judas experienced a self-perpetuating hell based on the energy of others. In reflecting upon my previous dream where I was damned to hell as Judas, I wonder what fueled the damnation? Did the words of others enter into Judas's thoughts where they festered and grew? Did people plant many seeds of damnation into his consciousness at the time of his death? What was the impact of millions of people over the last two millennia being taught to see Judas as a betrayer; was there a continuous planting of negativity into his consciousness?

After the *Gospel of Judas* was published, authors and academics have been writing a potentially more accurate depiction of Judas. What could this mean for the essence of Judas? If there is a more authentic story of Judas being written, does this lead to a restoration of him? If there is a restoration of Judas, is there a corresponding impact on the world; a dismantling of falsities, a shattering of structures, a crumbling of forces?

After this journey, I wondered more of what it meant to carry an unhealed aspect of Judas. If I had a fragment of his that carried the imprint of damnation and association of heavenly tasks with punishment, did this infiltrate my life? All my life, I assumed my feelings were mine. Now I was questioning this notion. It made me think of the movie *Lord of the Rings*, where whoever held the ring could be influenced by the ring's energy. Similarly, was I influenced by the essence of the fragment?

Looking back now, I better understand how this journey was additional preparation for the work to come with Judas. Along with being taken out of a tomb, given a name, the stigmata, and an energetic help button, I was taught how to view the consciousness of healing for the journeys yet to unfold. Though I did not know it at the time, this teaching laid the foundational altar for the healing work to come in future journeys. There would be no magic wands that would allow for the bypassing of the wisdom that has been buried in the wounds. There is a deliberate pealing of the proverbial onion necessary for the excavation of the truth and the liberation of the pain. If the onion were to disappear in a flash, as I sometimes wish pain would, then the wisdom of why the pain was present in the first place would be missed and the soul lesson not obtained. The complexity and the depth of the situation lie within the layers, not making the onion disappear.

A Journey of Surrender and Release

In this journey, I was a combination of Judas and myself. Together, we were going through a process of dying to old patterns and stored pain. The patterns and stored traumas were not explicitly named but energetically felt. I would feel an increase of energy that was rising to be transformed. As the energy built up, I knew I had to move into a crucifixion posture with my arms stretched out. By stretching out, the energy that had been building would transform and dissipate.

The crucifixion posture had nothing to do with being killed. It was a posture of complete openness and surrender, a posture of letting go. My feet being stationary meant there was no place to run to, no avoiding the transformation. My hands being motionless meant that there was nothing to be doing and fussing over. All that was left after my hands and feet were stationary was to be in my heart center.

I went through countless rounds of this process. As energy rose, I often trembled into the crucifixion posture. My body would shake, and much effort was required to move from a contracted position to an open and crucified posture. As I did, the energetics of the pattern / pain released. The pain being released looked like ghosts leaving my body one by one. After each release, I relaxed for a moment before another wave began. Each time, I moved back into the crucifixion pose for the process of dying of old traumas to proceed.

Sometimes, I had much resistance because the past traumas had to be felt for them to be healed. Feeling and being present to the vibrational frequencies of unhealed traumas was often uncomfortable. Though I knew the releases were bringing much freedom, I would often resist entering the next round.

Towards the end of this journey, there was ancestral healing for both Judas and me. The ancestors appeared as skeletons leaving our combined bodies, which led to the repairing of our DNA. At the end of this process, I saw a visual of a cross morphing into an Ankh. I knew this Ankh meant the completion of this process and signified the abundance of life force energy now available since much pain had been released.

Contemplations:

The crucifixion posture had nothing to do with being killed. This experience was a deep healing from a state of complete surrender. My arms being stretched was a posture of letting go of control, letting go of resistance, letting go of bearing a cross and carrying burdens in life, and most importantly, opening my heart. The release of old traumas was not a mental process of remembering as the healing was occurring. There was a remembrance of the feeling, not of actual events, as each layer was transforming. During the ancestral healing, I did not sense Judas and I were related. It was a shift from healing parts of ourselves to specifically healing what was coming down our individual the ancestral lines.

Healing the Heart of Judas

In this journey, I was Judas with some remembrance of being Kerry. While being Judas, I was to face my friend. I did not want to do this, but I knew I needed to. I was crying that such a deed was required. When I could finally make eye contact with my friend, all I saw was love. I witnessed the love of Creator in his eyes, and all tears instantly stopped. I heard a message from Spirit for my friend, "You are the love of Creator; you carry Creator's love in your daily life." Being witnessed by my friend allowed Judas to receive Divine Love.

I, as Judas, was then led to being witnessed over and over as Judas himself. For all those I presented myself to, all I received was love. I had a knowing of who I needed to present myself to, and I trembled upon knowing I was to be seen. I would reluctantly show myself, and the only response I received was love. For some people, I had to build up enormous courage to face them. Yet, as I would show myself and declare, "I am Judas," the response would always be, "I know, and I love you."

Through this process, Judas's heart was being healed. There was much healing and restoration in being witnessed. As people saw Judas, the Creator's love worked through them and shattered the walls around Judas's heart; the love blasted apart great boulders surrounding his being. The light and love transmitted by the witnesses ripped through the rock walls surrounding Judas's being.

Contemplations:

Judas repeatedly presents himself and is met only with love. This suggests that sometimes healing does not occur in isolation but through being witnessed in truth. This journey points to the possibility that Judas was experiencing a form of energetic restoration—a rebalancing of his legacy—though being witnessed. If he was condemned by humanity, then perhaps he must be seen by humanity in love to be restored.

Many shamanic traditions believe that we can send healing and witnessing across time—restoring balance to moments of wounding. Though, I was experiencing these journeys at the end of 2018, I might have been engaging with a part of his story that still exists in another layer of time or consciousness. If I was experiencing his need for help, it may be that I was stepping into a moment in time where he was struggling.

I came out of many journeys wondering why Judas would appear in my dreams and journeys as someone in need of support. Even if Judas, as a spiritual being, was in alignment with divine will, his name and essence have been burdened by millennia of projection, distortion, and vilification. He has been energetically exiled by humanity, trapped in a false narrative. From this perspective, my experiences may not be showing Judas himself in need of help, but rather the fragment of his story that remains misunderstood and unhealed in collective consciousness. It could be that I was encountering the pain of what has been placed upon him rather than his actual, liberated essence.

In many spiritual traditions, those who take on the role of a scapegoat carry enormous energetic weight. Even if Judas had fully accepted his role, it's possible that the sheer weight of collective judgment—over centuries—created a kind of spiritual burden that required restoration.

Some mystical traditions suggest that beings who take on such roles are not necessarily "trapped," but may require acknowledgment and witnessing in order to fully integrate what has been placed upon them. If Judas bore the weight of humanity's projections, my dreams may be serving as a point of reconciliation—helping him to be seen and understood in a way that was denied to him for so long.

Journeying with Judas led me to reflect on the role of the psychopomp—a spiritual guide, such as a shaman, healer, or ancestral spirit, who assists souls in transitioning beyond the physical world. If Judas died carrying unbearable sorrow, or if his name has been condemned for generations, an aspect of his energy may remain in an unresolved state. In this case, my experiences with Judas may not be about saving him personally, but rather about witnessing, guiding, and helping to unravel the heavy imprint of judgment placed upon him.

If an entire culture remembers someone as a betrayer, that collective belief may hold an aspect of their spirit in suffering. Healing happens through remembrance—when a soul is seen in its truth, acknowledged, and freed from false perceptions. Various traditions, from ancestral healing to Theosophy, suggest that spiritual work can help release lingering distortions. In this sense, my connection to Judas may be a form of ancestral or spiritual witnessing, allowing his essence to be freed from centuries of condemnation.

Theosophy introduces the concept of the astral shell—a fragment of a person's energy that lingers in lower realms when collective consciousness continues to project strong emotions onto them. If millions of people across centuries have projected betrayal, guilt, and condemnation onto him, an energetic imprint of his suffering may still circulate in the collective human psyche and an echo of his suffering may still exist in the astral plane. If so, my experiences may be less about rescuing Judas's soul and more about dismantling the false construct of his eternal damnation, and witnessing him in truth rather than distortion.

Across spiritual traditions, a common thread emerges: no soul is ever truly lost, but some aspects of consciousness can remain trapped due to unresolved emotions, karma, or collective perception. Whether Judas himself needed help, or whether his story needed redemption, remains an open question. Perhaps the final step in his journey is not his own salvation, but humanity's willingness to release him from the role of the eternal betrayer.

My experiences with Judas suggest that I may be engaging with an aspect of his energy that still seeks resolution. This does not mean that Judas as a soul is lost, but rather that: I was working with the energetic imprint of his suffering—whether from collective consciousness or a fragmented soul aspect; I was serving as a witness, allowing his truth to be restored beyond historical distortion; and/or I was acting as a psychopomp, helping to liberate his story from lingering misunderstandings.

A Reunion with Creator

In this journey, I witnessed Judas with Creator. Creator appeared as a shield made out of a three-dimensional geometric structure of white light, which was beautiful beyond words. This shield was dynamic and encircled Judas. Within this structure, Judas experienced a reunion with Creator. Judas allowed himself to be seen by Creator. The vision shifted to Judas drinking from Creator's cup. Judas received water from Creator and was quenching his thirst for life.

The journey shifted once more. Judas was standing in the safety of being seen 'in the middle.' This was not about being witnessed in a glorious way by Creator, nor was it about being seen as the devil. It was being seen 'in the middle' of a ginormous spectrum of all that is. In the middle was a void of all human constructs; this void brought spaciousness and expansiveness. Spirit said to Judas, "You see from the middle. You hold the middle."

<u>Contemplations:</u>

In this journey, nothing else was present but God's love. There was no fear of facing God, no worries about being assigned a great responsibility that would cost his life, no fear of punishment, no sense of shame. There was nothing present but God's love. No human mind constructs of this or that.

This notion of the 'middle' was introduced here and appeared again later with much more significance. In the middle was a void of all beliefs related to God and God's love for us. In the middle, there were no fears of being seen. Seeing from the center was the action of making duality weaker in force, content, and value as if duality was diffused while simultaneously experiencing the expansiveness of all that is.

This journey was transformative for me. Even though I have outgrown many of my childhood beliefs related to God and being worthy of God's love, this journey brought a deeper level of dissolving false beliefs. It brought up a fire of deconstruction of the very question that one can be or cannot be worthy of God's love. I grew up with this notion that God decides if we are worthy of his love and that he can turn on and off his love for us. In this journey, there was no space for such a concept to exist. In this journey, none of these constructs were present. It was not difficult to be seen, loved, and embraced by Creator. Being embraced by Creator's love dissolved all beliefs as if they never existed because, in that realm, they never did.

Receiving God's love has not always been easy for me. Being more and more present to God's love and receiving it has been a process of letting in love and letting go of all the reasons I believed I was unlovable. I believe that Creator sees us and loves us endlessly and eternally and that though we can feel separated from Creator, we can never truly be separated. For me, it is not a question if God loves us or not. The questions are can we be present and open to God's love, and can we allow ourselves to be witnessed and transformed by the power of love? I feel it is up to me to open my heart and receive the Creator's ever-present love.

In this journey, such a concept of opening or closing our hearts to God's love didn't exist. Reflecting upon this made me wonder where such a construct of closing our hearts and running from God originated. If one feels guilt and shame, why would one want to hide from God? It fundamentally makes zero sense to hide, close one's heart, from an Almighty Loving Presence that can help us heal the very feelings of unworthiness, unlovability, guilt, and shame. It makes more sense that it would be in our very nature to run to the Almighty; run at full speed into the embrace of love.

Judas's Life as Sacred and Holy

In this journey, I initially went through a sanctification process for myself, and then the process was related to Judas.

Spirit led me on an extensive journey. Spirit first asked, "Are you the firekeeper of your life?" I did not feel to be my own firekeeper; in fact, I never considered such a thing. Spirit guided me to see that I kept my fire in my foundation, my root. In my root was a bed of coals and a burning fire. This fire was love. I was in awe that this fire even existed. After being shown this foundation, Spirit guided me through a detailed process of discovering, acknowledging, and honoring where I held specific awarenesses and "medicines."

Spirit asked, "Where is your holiness?" I searched and found it in my womb. "Where is your connection to Creator?" I found my connection in my center. "Where is your power?" My power turned out to be in the same spot as my connection to God, in my center. My personal power and my relationship with God were intertwined and located in the same space. When I looked closely at my center, I saw a bundle of sage. As I breathed with my diaphragm, my breath fanned the sage into a protective smoke.

Spirit asked, "Where is the temple of heaven located in you?" After searching, I found it in my heart. "Where is your medicine of truth?" I found my medicine of truth located in my throat. My honor was held in my crown. My trust was situated in my third eye. I was confused on why trust would be located in my third eye. Spirit helped me realize that what I see in my journeys in my third eye can be trusted and then spoken through my throat, where my truth is anchored.

As the journey continued with Spirit asking for particular medicines, I continued to look. My lungs were my connection to the element of air, and my nostrils held my dragon breath of fire. My blood and lymph were my connection to the essence of water. My feet connected me to Earth. Honeybees lined my spine. My skin and hair held my preparedness, and the back of my neck had my safety. My aura and Merkabah held my sacredness. Light, compassion, joy, wisdom, love, knowing, and reverence made up every fiber of my being. A gold chalice in front of my spine and below my heart held my sacred marriage with Krishna. Lastly, there was a sword from Joan of Arc in my right hand as part of my medicine.

At the end of this extensive process, I wanted my back blessed by someone or some being other than me. Questions from Spirit arose: "Do you have your own back; do you trust yourself; do you not embody the holiness to do your own blessing; if you embody your holiness, does your back even need a blessing?" Spirit was not suggesting that it was not good to receive support from others, but rather challenging me to own my power.

The teachings continued to help me understand the holiness and sacredness of a Creator-infused life. There was not only a focus on our physical bodies as embodiments of creation, but also making everyday life sacred such as seeing and experiencing blankets as "Comforters." This was not to imply that something as mundane as a blanket was equivalent to Jesus, the "Comforter." It was a message to see the sacredness in all aspects of life, to infuse the sacredness into the mundane. This was not to worship the material world but to help feel the presence of God in the very fabric of our everyday lives.

Spirit asked me to imagine the impact of my holiness on others. I simply could not imagine such a thing, even after going through this process. Then Spirit said, "Claim your seat. Feel the sacredness of your seat. Be serious. Take the sacred seriously." It was not enough to find these "medicines" within me. It was necessary to claim them and consciously work with them.

After the completion of my experience, the focus turned to Judas. Spirit asked, "What would the impact of Judas's holiness have on others?" Spirit was asking me to see Judas's life as holy and to know the impact of his holiness. I heard the question, but I did not have an understanding nor an answer. However, I understood that I needed to go through this process of sanctification for myself first before I could even be asked such a question about Judas.

<u>Contemplations</u>:

I know the different chakras, energy centers, have unique purposes and functions and work together as a whole. Yet, I never considered different "medicines" being held in various locations within me and what them working together would mean. Within the journey of expanded awareness, it was easy for me to explore and be present with various medicines. After reentering this 3rd dimensional experience, I acknowledge there is much for me to embody fully and that this is an ongoing process for me.

I wonder if we each have our unique medicines and the way they are stored within us. Do we each have our unique medicine mandalas? I wonder how all these different medicines work together. When each part is recognized and worked with consciously, what foundation does that create for one's life and the impact they are here to have? Does the medicine we hold correspond to our life's purpose? When all of our medicines are activated, are we in alignment and can fulfill our purpose?

What is Judas's medicine mandala? What medicines does he hold? I reflected on my past-life regression where Jesus said, *"Do not consider Judas as Divine. Know him as Divine."* Many of the dominant stories told of Judas have not been stories based on his holiness. There have mostly been disparaging stories that lead him to be regarded as unacceptable, untrustworthy, and downright evil. Is Judas moving from being blacklisted, severely severed, and rejected, not only from our churches but from our hearts, to being witnessed as sacred and holy? In Judas's totality, in his complete medicine mandala, what would the impact of Judas's sacredness and holiness have on others?

The Mother of a Savior

In this journey, I was made aware that Judas's mother had a significant wound related to him. His mother denied him, resented him, and hated him. I questioned Spirit as I assumed that his mother, now in spirit form, would understand his role. I was corrected and told she needed healing, and their relationship needed healing as well.

I stepped into the role of Judas's mother. I was standing within a ceremonial space and saw Judas, as a young boy, running away from me. I called to him, but he did not return. I went after him but knew I must remain within the scared space. I could not leave the ceremony. It was important not to leave, and at the same time, go and get him. I went to the edge of the ceremonial grounds and then took one step outside. I was in between where Judas was and the center of the ceremony. Since I couldn't go any further, I made myself into a beacon of light so he could find me and return. He came crawling back, unwillingly. I took his hand and walked with him back into the ceremony. There was much work that needed to be done.

There was an altar in the middle of the ceremonial space. Judas's mother appeared. Since she was present, I stepped out of my role as Judas's mother. I went to the altar with his mother, as Judas waited nearby. His mother rewrote her story from being the mother of the soul who killed the only Son of God to a savior's mother. She, herself, sparked her Christed-self and became a Christed being. She had accepted her Christed-self as well as Judas's truth. Judas could then be present with his mother.

<u>Contemplations:</u>

In this journey, when I stepped into the role of his mother, I felt like a surrogate mother to Judas. I wonder if the essence of Judas's mother was working through me, similar to how people channel angels and ascended masters. Does being Roc-a-Sha enable me to work with his mother in this multidimensional way? Though I cannot answer this with absolute clarity, I can share that this did not feel symbolic nor metaphorical.

In this journey, Judas's mother went through a significant healing process and ignited her Christed-self. After which, Judas could be present with her and no longer felt the need to run. Future journeys, where Judas's mother appeared, were profoundly different from this one. It seemed that the healing in this experience allowed her to show up in support of Judas. Why was healing even in order?

Judas's mother played a role in later journeys, including the next one where she reminded him of why he was born. Was her role imperative in Judas's process? Was it essential that Judas's mother be in alignment with his truth? As a mother, was she assisting Judas in his 'rebirth' and the 'birth' of a new consciousness?

What Judas was Born to Do

In this journey, I was Judas's mother. I saw both Judas and Jesus playing together as children. I had a knowing that Judas needed to relive his childhood with Jesus. I left them alone to play until I had a feeling it was time to check-in on them. I sensed Judas was moments away from becoming completely unhinged. There was a kind of timelapse happening within his awareness. Judas was transitioning from his childhood innocence into his knowing of what he was born to do. He went from being carefree and playing to completely alert and vigilant. As the timeline played out in his awareness, the more unstable he became. As his mother, I told him he was courageous and reminded him why he was born. Judas calmed down and resettled into his childhood with Jesus.

Contemplations:

In this journey, Judas's mother knew his purpose and could remind him why he was born. How important was it for Judas's mother to understand his purpose and be the very one to remind him of what he was born to do? It felt like Judas was going through a rebirthing process and that his mother was assisting him with this. What would his rebirth herald, and how essential was the role of Judas's mother in his restoration?

From Fragmented to King

I was sitting by a fire and witnessed the appearance of Judas as well as many other people. Each person present held a fragment of Judas. These fragments were unhealed aspects of Judas. We all released and returned to Judas the element we had been carrying for him. This was a lot for Judas to process, yet we collectively knew it was
time, and he was capable of doing this profound healing. Spirit asked me to hold space and hold 'ground' for Judas as he had his ups and downs with the intensity of the process and as he found his way.

Judas had moments of being physically contorted; it looked like he was in severe pain as he processed the fragments. He was not in a purely physical form and had moments of disappearing into the ground and coming back. I was not to get drawn into any of his processes. I was to hold the image of Judas completely healed. He was integrating all the fragments, which included both wounds and the wisdom of the wounds. It was tumultuous at times.

As the intensity increased, I didn't think I could handle supporting Judas through the process. I realized I needed to hold space as Roc-a-Sha, and that this was part of my work. I was guided by Spirit not only to remain present and calm but to recognize Judas as healed. My main task at that moment was to remember him as healed and witness him as whole and in his glory. Within each fragment, there was wound energy and wisdom energy. There was much wisdom present, not as thoughts but as beautiful frequencies.

As the process continued, he appeared as pieces of gold and then briefly as a king. This was a process of him re-membering himself in his truth. Though that sounds wonderful, he was not comfortable with this, and he tried to hide in a cave-like tomb. I closed the cave so he could not enter and told him, "That is no longer an option." Then I saw a small spacecraft that symbolized his desire to leave Earth. I told Judas this is his realm and that he belongs here. I then understood my role to hold 'ground' for Judas as he anchored and claimed his place on Earth.

<u>Contemplations</u>:

Various spiritual traditions address soul fragmentation, integration, and transformation. Many indigenous and shamanic traditions believe that trauma causes soul fragmentation, where pieces of a person's soul become lost or dispersed across time and space. Soul retrieval ceremonies are performed to reclaim and reintegrate these lost aspects, restoring wholeness to the individual. In my journey, the people holding fragments of Judas and returning them to him closely mirrors this concept, suggesting that his essence had been scattered and required intentional reintegration.

In Jewish mysticism, particularly Kabbalistic thought, the concept of *Tikkun HaNefesh* (soul repair) and *Tikkun Olam* (repair of the world) emphasizes the healing of both the individual and the collective. If Judas's soul was fractured by the weight of misunderstanding and condemnation, the act of returning his fragments could be seen as a cosmic correction—restoring not just him, but also an essential truth that has been distorted over time.

The themes in my journey also resonate with Hindu and Buddhist ideas of rebirth. In these traditions, past actions create energetic imprints that influence one's present and future experiences. The intense process Judas underwent—painful, tumultuous, yet ultimately transformative—suggests a form of resolution. His oscillation between struggle and golden light reflects a spiritual alchemy, where wounds are transmuted into wisdom, and suffering gives way to a higher state of being.

This journey also reflected the collective nature of healing. If multiple individuals carried fragments of Judas, were we all karmically linked to him? I wondered if these people had similar experiences to me. Did they have similar dreams? Who were these people? Had I crossed paths with any of them and not known it? Were we all from this timeline? Who were we to take on such a task? Was this a part of our destiny? What would have happened if we failed in our mission to return the fragments we carried?

More significantly, does this imply that the belief in his betrayal was so deeply embedded in human consciousness that it required multiple people to process and return these pieces? This raises profound questions about the nature of wounds—not only as personal burdens but as collective imprints that persist across time.

This journey also explores the relationship between suffering and wisdom. The returned fragments contained not only pain but also knowledge, which was present as beautiful frequencies rather than mere thoughts. This suggests that suffering itself may hold an intrinsic wisdom, but it is only through integration that this wisdom is revealed.

A puzzle can be broken into pieces, then reassembled, and remain at the same level of consciousness. When soul fragments come back, do they simply return, or do they come back with enhanced wisdom? If soul fragments return carrying past misunderstandings or false narratives, does their reintegration elevate consciousness beyond its previous state? In other words, does this kind of soul retrieval restore things to the way they were, or does it birth something entirely new?

His transformation into golden light and then into a king symbolizes empowerment, redemption, and a new role. Does his resurrection signify not just personal healing, but a planetary shift in understanding? If he is reclaiming his place, what long-lost truth is being restored, and how might it reshape the consciousness of humanity?

Judas's integration is possibly about far more than his personal wholeness—it may be about the resurrection of wisdom that has long been obscured. His journey from fragmentation to kingship challenges centuries of perception, hinting at a greater purpose beyond betrayal and redemption. If his wounds contained essential knowledge, and if his resurrection was not just for himself but for the world, then perhaps his true role has yet to be fully understood.

Cleaning up Hell

I was Judas's mother in this journey. I saw the area of hell that Judas had resided in and instinctively knew that it needed to be cleaned with light. As his mother, I felt a desire to do the cleaning for him. I sat down in the darkness of his previous cell and called upon my strength and my light. I was not afraid. I felt the darkness of hell closing in on me, so I anchored myself as a beacon. I knew not to take this lightly, as I was in the consciousness of hell.

I was in the process of cleaning Judas's cell for him, but then I was not allowed. Judas had to do this. I was quickly shown a chick hatching from an egg as a metaphor. I knew that if you help a chick out of its eggshell, it can die in the process of hatching. Part of the hatching process is strengthening its neck muscles as it pecks away at the shell. If you help too much, the neck muscles do not develop, and the chick will die because the neck muscles are too weak to hold up its head. In the quick moment of seeing the egg, I knew the cleaning was for Judas to do. Though I had no idea why this needed to be done, I knew it was not my process.

Judas and Jesus appeared. Jesus and I, as Judas's mother, held space for Judas as he blasted light into the cell. I thought this might take a while, so I prepared myself to settle in for a lengthy process. Yet, it took Judas no time at all. It was not a process of forty days in the desert. It was a forty second process. I chucked to myself at how speedy Judas was.

After the process was complete, we exited the cell. I went to close the cell door so no other souls could reside there. Spirit told me that I do not have permission to do this. If a soul needs this experience, the door is open.

<u>Contemplations</u>:

Was this cell a state of consciousness as well as a place within the space / time continuum? What does it mean that Judas's cell needed to be cleaned? As his mother, I wanted to nurture him and take care of him. I was willing to enter a state of hell for him, without questioning or a moment of hesitation. What a love! Yet, I was to hold space as I had done in the previous journey as Judas integrated his fragments. This time I was his mother, instead of Roc-a-Sha. Was his mother necessary because mothers have responsibilities to teach children many lessons, including working through pain? The image of the egg indicated it would have been enabling and even harmful for Judas if I cleaned for him, as opposed to holding space, which was strengthening for him.

I knew the number 40 was symbolic and not literal. The number 40 appears frequently in the Bible and is often associated with testing, transformation, purification, and preparation for a new phase of spiritual growth. It signifies a period of trial that leads to renewal or a deeper connection with God.

Jesus fasted 40 days in the desert (Luke 4:2). The time between the resurrection of Jesus to Jesus's ascension was also forty days (Acts 1:3). During the flood, rain fell for 40 days and 40 nights (Genesis 7:4). The Israelites wandered in the desert for 40 years as a test of faith before entering the Promised Land (*Numbers 14:33-34*). Moses spent 40 days and nights on Mount Sinai receiving the Law (*Exodus 24:18*), highlighting a time of divine instruction and transformation. Elijah journeyed for 40 days to Mount Horeb, where he encountered God and received guidance (*1 Kings 19:8*).

Overall, the number 40 represents a sacred interval—a period of divine testing, refinement, and renewal. Whether through trials, purification, or preparation for a higher calling, the biblical significance of 40 underscores the transformative journey toward spiritual awakening and fulfillment.

In this experience, it was significant to me that the time was not in days or years but seconds. It took no time at all. Judas felt ready, in alignment, and powerful. He was not going to belabor this task, nor was it arduous for him. There was no figuring out how to clean his cell, nor any difficulty in doing so. This cell, this level of consciousness, was complete.

Turtle

In this cluster of journeys, I was often a large turtle. Sometimes, I was on my back, completely surrendered, and rocking on my rounded shell. It was quite enjoyable and brought me much delight. I was never bothered by being on my back and unable to right myself to my feet. I never felt trapped or stuck in this surrendered state. I felt like a child rocking with joy.

The upper shell represented heaven. The underside symbolized Earth. While being on my back, the bottom shell was sending Earth to heaven, and the lower shell was anchoring heaven on Earth. My essence, being in the middle of the shells, was uniting heaven and Earth. All I needed to do for this to happen was be surrendered in this pose, as an upside-down turtle.

As I was there, in-between the shells, I held the energy of 'the middle.' I was experiencing the 'medicine of the middle,' the medicine that Judas carries. I was to understand Judas's place in all of creation; to apply the medicine of Judas in my life; hold the understanding of his teachings in my heart, and be true to myself.

<u>*Contemplations:*</u>

When the turtle would appear in my visions, it gave me moments of embracing the medicine of the middle; embracing all from a middle, central, non-dualistic, expansive point. In later journeys, this medicine of the middle evolved into being symbolized by an infinity symbol.

I thought back to my past-life regression, where this same notion of connecting heaven and Earth was present. What did this mean? As I wondered before, aren't these two realms always connected? Was the turtle providing a clue? The turtle reminded me of Native American creation stories in which the turtle was present at Earth's creation.

Many indigenous people view turtles as symbolic of not only creation but also of truth.

It is interesting to contemplate the journey when Spirit asked where was my connection to Creator; where was my power. My power turned out to be in the same spot as my connection to Creator, in my center. My power and my connection to Creator were intertwined and located in the same space, my middle.

Death of Judas

In this journey, I watched the events of Judas's death unfold. I saw people throw his body into a ditch and smashed it with stones. They were uncontrollable.

I recognized one of the souls of the people in the crowd of angry followers. I recognized her as someone I know from this lifetime. She was in a different physical form, and yet I knew it was her.

<u>Contemplations:</u>

Though I have no attachment to how Judas died, I do have a devotion to the truth. I also have a deep curiosity on why, if his death was fabricated in biblical scripture, what purpose in our human evolution did this fabrication serve? It is worth noting that there are inconsistencies in what the biblical literature says about Judas's death. In Mathew, it indicates that Judas hung himself. In Acts, Judas burst open, and his insides came pouring out. In Papias, there is a legendary account that Judas enlarged into a humongous being; a doctor could not locate his eyes, and his urine was filled with pus and worms, among other grotesque details.

The truth about how Judas or anyone dies is significant. If Judas was murdered, why did biblical authors fabricate Judas's death as a suicide or spontaneous combustion? Was the fabrication of his death as a suicide more than just covering an ugly truth of him being brutally murdered; was his death rewritten to hide something, a mystery? I also wonder about the significance of a proper burial of the body after one passes. Does an improper burial of the body have any effect on the soul? If Judas's body was indeed thrown into a ditch, what impact did that have on his essence?

In my past-life regression, Archangel Michael told me the noose was not "linked to anything valid." Was he saying there was no link, no association between Judas hanging himself with a noose, and the truth of Judas's death? The noose not being linked to anything could have meant there was no connection or relatedness between biblical literature on Judas's death and how he actually died. In my second dream, I was damned to hell as Judas and saw people above my grave throwing stones onto me. In that dream, I did not perceive any message about how Judas died as the focus was on reversing damnation.

This journey was straightforward and clear. Judas was killed; I had vivid images of the angry mob that stoned him. At the time, I was not surprised to receive such information. However, a month or so after this experience, I was amazed to read in the *Gospel of Judas* that Judas shared with Jesus a vision he had of his death. In the vision, Judas saw himself being stoned to death by the disciples. Jesus tells Judas that he has seen his fate. By following the orders of Jesus, Judas will be hated and persecuted by the other disciples (Judas 45). It was to my astonishment that there was any information in historical literature that was even remotely correlated to the message I received.

Freeing the Souls who Killed Judas

Before I detail this journey, I feel it is necessary to provide some background to the Sundance Ceremony that I saw in my visions. The Sundance is a sacred ceremony practiced by the Lakota and Plains Native Americans. The annual ceremony is a time of renewal for people and the Earth. For the four-day ceremony, a circular arbor is constructed, and a large cottonwood tree is placed in the center. Dancers participate in the ceremony as Eagle Dancers or Line Dancers. Eagle Dancers choose to be tethered to the tree via a piercing. Some Eagle Dancers pierce the skin on their chest with a carved twig or a slender animal bone. A rope from the tree is then attached to their piercing, which allows them to be tethered to the tree for the ceremony. Other Eagle Dancers choose to have a deeper piercing through their chest muscles. This deeper piercing allows the dancers to hang from the piercing with their feet off the ground as they pray. Line Dancers dance with their feet on the ground in a circle around the cottonwood tree. I have done this ceremony as a Line Dancer and never as an Eagle Dancer. In this journey, I was doing both at the same time.

In this journey, Judas and I were in a combined state; two souls in one body. We were participating in a Sundance ceremony. There were two sets of us, in two different locations in the ceremonial arbor. One was an Eagle Dancer, and the other was a Line Dancer. As an Eagle Dancer, we were hanging from a piercing through our chest muscles, with our feet off the ground, from the Tree of Life. As the Line Dancer, we stood on the earth next to an elder and looked at ourselves as the Eagle Dancer.

As an Eagle Dancer, we were hanging to free the souls who killed Judas. There was no separation or distinction between Judas and me. Together, Judas and I were making a sacrifice to free the souls of those who killed him. As the journey progressed, there was an image of Judas's grave. Stones that were used to kill Judas were vanishing from the grave.

<u>Contemplations</u>:

The Sundance ceremony is a significant part of my life. It was interesting to see the Sundance appear in my vision as I don't relate Native American traditions with Judas's time period. Regardless, what was important was the sacrifice being made to free the souls. This journey supported the understanding that Judas was killed and added to the account the impact on the souls who committed the deed. The souls of those who killed Judas were being freed. What place / dimension / level of consciousness were they being released from, and what caused them to be stuck?

The cottonwood tree in the center of the dance arbor is considered to be the Tree of Life. It is not just a symbol or a metaphor, but an actual tool used by the dancers to connect with Great Spirit. In the journey, we were tethered to the Tree of Life to make a sacrifice. Though we were tethered, as dancers are in actual ceremonies, there was profound freedom and a sense of liberation and expansiveness as the souls were being freed. As we hung from the Tree of Life, with a piercing through our chest muscles, there was healing for us as we made the sacrifice for others, the very ones that killed Judas. There was a connectedness in our humanity that transcended time and space. We were all healing together. There was a collective pain that we were transmuting through our prayers and sacrifices.

Black Sheep Birthing Sacred Lambs

In this dream, Spirit was teaching me about the relationship between black sheep and sacred lambs. Spirit emphasized that black sheep are the misfits of society; misfitting, not fitting in, not being a part of the flock is good as it allows for patterns to be broken. The new consciousness that can arise from breaking free of societal customs was represented as the sacred lamb.

Symbolically, Spirit stressed that black sheep make sacrifices by breaking patterns or cycles, and in doing so, they initiate change. To create lasting change, a black sheep needs to do more than break away from the old; it must bring forth the lamb. The offspring of the black sheep, the sacred lamb, must be raised in the new consciousness to bring about lasting change. In this dream, metaphorically, lambs anchored in a new awareness and level of consciousness.

Contemplations:

It is interesting to contemplate that it may not be sufficient to break away from the pack to end a family pattern or societal programming. To spark and truly birth the new consciousness and make lasting change, a sacred lamb needs to be born. In the *Gospel of Judas*, there is mention of Jesus separating Judas from the other disciples. After he was separated, Jesus shared the mysteries of the heavens with Judas. In that regard, Judas was a black sheep. He was removed, not part of the flock, and from this point of separation, he was given teachings the others did not hear. Judas was the black sheep of the apostles; he stood apart from them.

Perhaps Judas can be viewed as a lamb as well. Through a biblical lens, lambs represent a sacrifice. Did Judas sacrifice his life? If he knew the followers of Jesus would kill him, he died a martyr, and his life was a sacrifice. If Judas did sacrifice his life because he believed in Jesus and the mission Jesus laid out for him, what was the sacred lamb, the consciousness, of which Judas gave birth?

I was taught that sacrifices are offered to make something sacred and holy. We sacrifice a meal to make food and the act of eating more sacred. We give something up, not for loss, but to enhance sacredness. Through this lens of sacrifice, what did the death of Judas make sacred?

Deliverance Through Betrayal

I heard the words from Spirit, "Rewrite the kiss." Infused in these words was an understanding that the biblical story of the betrayal was not written correctly. I saw the word betray broken apart into two words: 'be' and 'tray.' The breaking of the word betray also broke its meaning. Spirit broke down this word into two parts, breaking down its historical meaning and breaking down all the beliefs held within. What arose from the breaking was a new consciousness of deliverance. The word 'tray' was symbolic of deliverance because we carry and deliver items on trays. Though we would never deliver a human on a tray, at this moment, it was a symbol. The word "be" was emphasized: 'be' a deliverer; 'be' the consciousness of deliverance.

<u>Contemplations:</u>

The story of Judas betraying Jesus with a kiss has infiltrated many aspects of our culture, including the visual arts, theater, literature, and music. Through the story of the kiss, Judas became an archetype of betrayal and was marked as one of the most notorious traitors in history. He is seen as not only a shadowy figure but the actual embodiment of evil. Some deem Judas, the insider who turned on his master, the evil villain, as the only person who cannot be forgiven. The 'Judas Kiss' has even taken on a cultural meaning to refer to an act of appearing to be a friend who has malicious ulterior motives.

Some biblical historians believe that there is no historical evidence of Judas's deed and that his betrayal was fabricated (Pagels, E. H., & King, K. L., 2008, p. 29). If a fabrication was written, why? What was the purpose / intention behind telling the story of betrayal? What was the impact on the psyche of Christians and the collective consciousness?

I reflected on the time I had the fleeting thought, *"I think we have the story of Judas wrong. He was not a betrayer."* The consciousness of betrayal and the consciousness of deliverance are vastly dissimilar. It is interesting to note that the Greek word used in the Bible to describe the so-called betrayal is *paradidomi.* The translation of paradidomi is to hand someone over to another person; to transmit; to surrender.

Paradidomi does not hold the ethical condemnation that has been assigned to in when translated into English within Judas's context. Though the word paradidomi is used in other places in the New Testament, it is never used in a way to suggest a betrayal. For example, Paul used paradidomi to indicate that he handed over information to the Corinthians (Ehrman, 2006, p. 16).

Do we need to betray something / someone in order to be resurrected? If the betrayal was fabricated, do we need to betray this falsity to be renewed in the truth?

It is interesting to think about how I have used the word betrayal when speaking about breaking family patterns. I have expressed that when we need to break away from family rituals, it can feel like a betrayal to the family. By not adhering to established norms, it can feel more than letting them down but actually betraying them. As the black sheep of my family, I have felt that parting from family customs was a betrayal to the family system, not merely a natural part of growing up and doing my own thing. Since I have experienced how betraying specific family structures feels like liberation and freedom, I can feel how deliverance can be embedded in betrayal.

I have often thought about the bible passage where Jesus said he was here to bring a sword to cleave father from son and mother from daughter (Matthew 10:34-36). I have taken this to mean that Jesus came to help us break free of what has been coming down the generations in the form of beliefs and unhealthy behavioral patterns. If breaking a family pattern is a form of betrayal, perhaps not all betrayals are bad. Symbolically, could cleaving father from son be the cleaving of a false god (father) from the humans (sons) who worship him? Could cleaving mother from daughter be about sorting out the differences between the falsies about our origins and the true mother of creation?

Were we betrayed? Were we misled by a falsified story of the betrayal, and if so, why? Are we being called to betray the system, to betray the stories that we have been told, to be blasphemous, be heretical? I can imagine that many would call me a heretic for even questioning the story of the betrayal. I don't feel this is a matter of differing opinions from what has been determined by church authority as unquestionably true, but a deep searching of where revealed truth (truth believed to be revealed from God) truly originates. Being heretical, being at odds with what has been generally accepted as truth, might bring a greater understanding that will lead to a deeper level of freedom — deliverance through betrayal.

If we are to betray and reject the 'truth' handed down to us, how do we know we have not accessed another fabricated story? How do we distinguish between falsified information and knowledge / wisdom? How do we navigate towards the truth within the structures of information claiming truth, yet they are not of truth? How do we sort through the many constructs that are embedded into our culture and the collective mind? I believe it is our responsibility to discern what we accept as accurate and have faith that the illusion of any false aspects of our reality will be illuminated as we gain wisdom. This wisdom might come through an act of betraying what has been handed down to us.

Laurels

Spirit said multiple times, "The laurels." Spirit emphasized the plural of the word laurels, and I understood that there were at least two beings that the symbol of the laurels represented. In my heart, I knew that one of the laurels related to Judas. I thought about what laurels symbolized. I acknowledged them as symbols of the resurrection of Christ, eternal glory, and truth. They also represent triumph, victory, and the end of a conflict. Associating the laurels with Judas symbolized his truth, triumph over hell; it was symbolic of his true essence and eternal life in heaven. Though I did not obtain specific information, I could sense that Judas marked the end of a conflict and initiated a new era.

<u>Contemplations:</u>

In a previous journey, I briefly saw Judas as a king; therefore, associating Judas with laurels, or even a crown of laurels felt appropriate as his true essence, to me, is mighty, powerful, and divine. I sensed the end of a conflict in the journey and wondered what conflict Judas brings to completion. Is it an internal conflict, a global conflict, a battle of faith, a struggle between the true and false gods?

Is it a dispute related to the truth of Judas's life, death as well as his purpose? What new era could Judas initiate?

This message implied two beings, and yet no information came to me in the journey. Upon reflection, I believe that Spirit wanted me to associate the laurels with Judas and Mary Magdalene. In my past-life regression, a similarity was made between Judas and Mary, as they were both falsely labeled. The original biblical story of Mary was rewritten by Pope Gregory the Great in the 6th century. In a sermon, he fused three New Testament women into Mary Magdalene: Mary Magdalene with the seven demons; the unnamed sinner who washed Jesus's feet with her hair (Luke); and Mary of Bethany, who anoints Jesus with nard (John). In this one act, Pope Gregory portrayed Mary Magdalene as a prostitute.

The Catholic Church redacted this conclusion in 1969, thirteen hundred years after the Pope's sermon. Though the decree was redacted, many still believe Mary was the sinner Gregory made her out to be. In the early 1980s, as I was raised in the Catholic Church, I was taught that Mary was a prostitute redeemed by Jesus. This legend has held great tenacity regardless of the redaction. It illustrates the power of one Pope to alter the perception of people around the world. His sermon was hundreds of years after Mary lived and had a ripple effect of over thirteen hundred years into the future.

If one Pope could rewrite Mary's story, what is the possibility that one oral storyteller altered Judas's story in such a way that influenced New Testament authors? What if an oral storyteller, who felt betrayed by a family member, changed Judas's story to express his feelings through a narrative? What if an altered account was then passed down the generations and influenced New Testament authors?

Reflecting on Mary, I wonder if we have misunderstood the biblical passages about her. For example, Luke 8:2 and Mark 16:9 state that Jesus exorcised "seven demons" from her. But are we certain these demons represented evils or sins? What if the so-called "demons" symbolized the limiting beliefs imposed on women by the dominant culture? Perhaps Jesus wasn't casting out literal demons but rather freeing Mary from societal constraints. And if she did have inner demons, could confronting them have been a transformative process—one that made her a powerful healer, capable of helping others face and overcome their own inner struggles?

Recently, gnostic scholarship has brought to light potentially more historically accurate portrayals of Mary. The *Gospel of Mary* portrays her as a beloved disciple of Jesus who had a great capacity for understanding Jesus's teachings. Likewise, the *Gospel of Judas* has provided an alternative view of Judas.

Another gnostic text worth mentioning is the *Gospel of Thomas* written by Didymus Judas Thomas. Both names, Didymus and Thomas, mean twin: Didymus is Greek for twin, and Thomas is Aramaic. I wonder if the same author wrote the *Gospel of Thomas* and the *Gospel of Judas* as the similarities between the texts are intriguing. My point is not to provide a detailed analysis of the texts' similarities, but to question if we have been so conditioned to believe Judas was a traitor that there is little room in our psyche to consider that he could have been the primary influence of the *Gospel of Thomas*? Both the *Gospel of Thomas* and the *Gospel of Judas* have a similar gnostic theology. Both accounts start with the mentioning that the gospels share the "secret words" (Thomas) and the "secret account" (Judas) of Jesus's teachings.

In both gospels, Judas and Thomas are the closest disciples to Jesus, who were the only ones to understand where Jesus came from and the only ones to receive the secret mysteries from Jesus. In both gospels, there is a similarity of being stoned by the other disciples. Judas had a vision of being stoned to death, and Thomas writes that if he told the others what Jesus shared with him that they would "pick up stones and throw them" at him. Has the story of Judas deeply penetrated our consciousness, preventing us from considering the possibility that Judas could have bestowed such knowledge and passed it along where it was held within the oral traditions until written down in the *Gospel of Thomas*.

Mary Magdalene and Judas Iscariot have been framed as the prostitute and the betrayer. They have been incorrectly depicted in classical art and literature, made into archetypes that are not historically accurate. What is the long-term impact of inaccurate portrayals on Judas and Mary as well as those brought up within these erroneous teachings? What was Spirit asking me to understand by associating the laurels, a symbol of the resurrection of Christ, eternal glory, and truth, with Judas and Mary? Together, are Judas and Mary ending a conflict, a misalignment with truth?

True God and False Gods

I was looking at the Earth from afar as if I was floating in outer space. Encircling the Earth was an energetic encasing that I could see in a yellowish gold color. To the left of the Earth was a straight beam of white light that reached far into space.

There was a distinction made between the True God and the false gods. The false gods fabricated the Earth. The yellowish-gold color around Earth was a false heaven. The white beam of light to the left of Earth was the passageway to the True God and True Heaven.

Souls on Earth were separated into two groups: those that could not exit the false Earth and those that could. If souls could not exit, they entered the fabricated heaven after death and then reincarnated back to Earth. These souls existed within a closed system of the fabricated Earth and false heaven.

If a soul could leave the fabricated Earth after death, they accessed the white beam of light that reached far into space. This beam of light could take them to the True God and the True Heaven. There was no judgment about the different souls. One group was not better than the other, just different as one group was capable of exiting the fabricated Earth while others could not.

I was being shown where specific souls came from: they were from the True God and would return to the True God, or they were created by the sub-god and would stay within the Earth's sphere. The souls from the sub-god could not reach the beam of light and ascend to the upper heavenly realms. The souls created by the sub-god were like programs living within the matrix of the Earth and fabricated heaven. As Spirit showed me where specific souls came from, there was no judgment, only information.

Contemplations:

At the time of this journey, I was baffled at the possibility of Earth being fabricated by false gods. I was even more surprised to learn later that gnostic gospels, including the *Gospel of Judas,* talk about this notion of false gods and even have names for them, such as Saklas and Yaldabaoth. Gnostic texts are thought to originate from the early centuries of Christianity. The texts are varied yet emphasized the importance of 'gnosis' or knowing in order to transcend this material world, which according to Gnostics, is a faulty creation. The gnostic literature describes Earth as a creation of the false gods, a miserable world of suffering, and a cosmic disaster. These false gods are not only inferior and foolish but also bloodthirsty.

Gnostic writings are less about faith and more about knowledge. The gnosis or knowledge for salvation comes from a divine being who originates in the highest levels of heaven called the Pleroma. The Gnostics think that if we know the truth, the truth can literally set us free from this material world that was not created by the ultimate, True God, but from false, ignorant gods who entrap souls within their faulty creation (Ehrman, 2006, p. 57-59).

In the *Gospel of Judas*, there is mention of the god of this world not being the True God or God of Jesus. In a passage,

Jesus differentiated between his God and the god his disciples worship. Jesus laughed at his disciples, who were offering a prayer of thanksgiving to the false god. They are confused about why Jesus was laughing because they believed that what they were doing was correct. They asked, *"Master, why are you laughing at [our] prayer of thanksgiving? We have done what is right."* He answered and said to them, *"I am not laughing at you. <You> are not doing this because of your own will but because it is through this that your god [will be] praised."* The disciples are perplexed that Jesus differentiated between his god and their god. *They said, "Master, you are [...] the son of our god" (Judas 34).* In the *Gospel of Judas*, Jesus not only made a distinction between his God and the god the disciples mistakenly worship, but he declared their god to be an inferior, ignorant deity.

In my journey, there were two heavens, as well as two different kinds of humans: those who stayed within the sphere of the Earth and those who could access the True Heaven. In the *Gospel of Judas*, Judas was curious about the different kinds of human beings and asked Jesus who could attain ultimate salvation. Jesus answered by saying that some people have only a temporary existence, while others have eternal life. Jesus differentiated between the mortals who ignorantly worship a false creator and immortals who know the True God and the truth about the world. Those with a divine spirit will transcend the material world and live in the great realm above (Judas 44). In my vision, I did not get a sense of why certain souls stayed and others could leave. The gnostic literature states that people will be able to leave if they have knowledge / gnosis. The gnostic goal is not to stay here but to transcend this faulty creation, return to our heavenly home, and reunite in the upper divine realms with other eternal beings.

Though I find it fascinating that gnostic texts such as the *Gospel of Judas* refer to this notion of true and false gods, I feel there is a mystery still to be understood. What is a false god? Before this journey, I only considered how we can enter into a perpetual state of worshiping false gods such as money and celebrities and how enthralled, charmed, hypnotized, and enchanted we can get by whatever it is we are praising. I never considered that there could be a grander, cosmic false deity who created Earth and fabricated a heaven. From all the scientific and religious theories I have heard about Earth's creation, this notion of a false god creating Earth was new for me.

It feels impossible to completely comprehend the nature of reality and the existence of all that is. I wonder if there are insights to be gained from religious teachings around the world. Are diverse belief systems pointing to the notion of true and false gods, simple from other perspectives and using different terms? Does the Gnostic's concept of a true and false god relate to the Hindu's belief that the world is an illusion called Maya? Since Maya is considered separate from God, the eternal reality, there seems to be a correlation between truth and fiction, reality and illusion. Buddhists have a similar construct of freeing oneself from samsara and any attachments.

Is the concept of being plugged into the matrix the same as believing in false gods, swimming in samsara, and living within Maya? Some say the matrix is a computer-generated, holographic universe projected onto us, that we do not exist at base reality, but within a fabricated computer simulation. Within the simulation, we are manipulated into suppressing our true abilities and infinite powers.

This would feel very abstract to me, except that I had an experience in 2012 that I cannot make sense of, nor can I dismiss. One afternoon as I entered my living room, I saw my wall made out of green 0s and 1s streaming downward just as in the movie, *The Matrix*. The 0s and 1s streamed for only a few seconds, and then my wall became solid again. Though I cannot comprehend my experience, I am not quick to conclude from a few seconds of my life that what I saw meant all of creation was computer-generated, though it very well might be.

Though I have no conclusions about the notion of the false gods or a matrix, I speculate that they might be pointing to the same thing: an alignment to a particular level / field of consciousness. Some consider that everything in the 3rd dimension has a supportive, energetic field. Energetic fields can exist for everything from molecules to galaxies, including inanimate objects like crystals and rocks, to beings like plants, animals, and humans. Within each energetic field, information is stored as vibrational frequencies. Energetic fields are understood to hold the codes of form and function and, therefore, are likely to strongly influence how an object or being behaves. In other words, what we see in the 3rd-dimensional reality, a crystal, for example, originates from a subtle energetic vibration that then gives rise to the physical expression.

The aforementioned premise seems to be illustrated in a number of contexts. For example, essential oils have a supportive, energetic field of vast awareness that endorses their functions in the 3rd dimension. Likewise, a wellness modality, like massage, has an energetic field that holds the wisdom and consciousness of the modality. Some believe that ascended masters have diverse fields of consciousness that we, as humans, can directly or indirectly interact with.

Some speculate that fields of consciousness are dynamic and, therefore, can contract or expand. People can feed energy to these fields and make them larger: if many people use essential oils, the energetic field of essential oils grows; if we pray to a guru, we can expand the field of the guru. Yet, this does not mean that the fields' natural tendencies to continue to evolve may not be tainted by human thoughts that are not innate to the field. Dominant and collective human patterns may feed and enhance or deplete and distort a field of consciousness.

Suppose a collective of people can feed, enhance, and even taint a field. In that case, I wonder if, individually and collectively, we have been feeding the fields of Jesus, Judas, and Mary Madelene with energy in the form of untrue stories. Is it possible that we created fields that we are interacting with instead of connecting with the true essence of these beings?

I imagine that there are countless fields of consciousness available to us, and we have the option to tap into various ones at different times. I envision this to be similar to watching one television channel while multiple other channels exist. As each television station has unique programming, I imagine each field of consciousness has its characteristics and vibration. If a field of consciousness has features of x, y, and z, then when people tap into that field, they can begin to accept and exhibit the vibration / thoughts / behaviors of x, y, and z. Perhaps, when we tap into and entrain to a field, we are programmed and conditioned to frequencies of that field that then, in turn, establish and regulate specific kinds of thoughts and behaviors.

Suppose a field of consciousness is encoded with trickery related to spirituality. If we entrain into that field, we might experience a level of deception and, therefore, entrapment due to the consciousness embedded into that field. I have met many people who believe they are 'free' and have entered an enlightened plane of existence. Yet, I wonder if they have been disillusioned because they have tapped into a field laden with false light, a deceptive field that tells them they have arrived at a state of enlightenment. Subsequently, they feel that there is no illusion to transcend because the field they are tapped into conditions the mind to think they are awake and sovereign beings.

Can we have a false sense of breaking free? How do we know we have moved up in consciousness and not just over to a similar consciousness that is merely well-disguised as freedom? Perhaps we can exit one field / matrix and enter another, which is similar yet well disguised.

If a field of consciousness encoded with deception does exist, from where did it originate? Have we constructed fields with our collective consciousness? Perhaps we unconsciously co-create fields to have specific experiences; we tap into a field to learn, and when we've completed lessons, we emerge with the wisdom we have gained. I wonder if we are the matrix makers and if we are also the ones plugging in ourselves. To loosen the grip the matrix has on us, do we need to release our own grip? Perhaps we need to open the prison we built around ourselves; deconstruct the consciousness we may have created.

Is there something on Earth that is the by-product of a false god or matrix that we can tangibly see, evaluate, and through studying it, can better grasp the intangible, invisible nature of a false god or matrix? The notion of a matrix does not feel abstract to me when I look at the impact technology, especially social media, has on people. I ponder the possibility that the matrix and social media could be the 'me and mini-me' of the technological world. If under 100 designers could create the social media platform that impacted two billion people worldwide, could a handful of people make a matrix that has global consequences?

I have listened to people speak about how, to them, social media is designed in a way that encourages people to think and behave in a particular fashion. They believe social media has been effective in programming unconscious habits, conditioning people to be hooked and addicted, which, in turn, can impact one's free will. They also feel that the platform was built to be a tool, yet some seem to have become enslaved by the manipulation-based technology. They also believe that the impact of social media on us can be unnoticeable as we don't see the gradual change in our behavior and perception. When I listened to them speak, it felt so similar to my contemplations about a possible matrix. Can an undetectable matrix persuade what we do, how we think, and how we feel, keeping us entrained, entranced, and entrapped without us even knowing? Perhaps our freedom is in our ability to detect the undetectable.

In further contemplation, I thought about how social media was constructed by people and is now run by supercomputers, artificial intelligence with machine learning capabilities. As people built social media with algorithms that have a mind of their own, did people build a matrix as an advanced technology with a consciousness of its own, with an ability to change and advance itself, with processing power beyond human ability?

I can see that my contemplations about social media are about trying to understand the abstractness of a false god or matrix by looking at something very tangible. Social media creates micro-worlds where people can design their reality with their own set of facts. Within each microcosm, people can gain a false sense that their world and set of facts are those of the majority and falsely believe that many others agree with them and their notions of reality. We can be operating on a different set of facts and concepts of reality while rejecting information that contradicts our perceived and constructed worldview. What is true depends upon the microcosm they have created. People who believe the Earth is flat are perhaps not uneducated as much as they are educated within a field of consciousness. What's real and true depends not upon fact but upon field.

I imagine that there is a great possibility that there is an incalculable number of fields of collective consciousness that support our various notions of reality. I feel Judas Iscariot and Mary Magdalen help us understand the complexity of the consciousness of religious doctrine and how it relates to human conditioning. I have met people who are convinced that they know Judas's story correctly and believe with 100% certainty that Mary was a prostitute.

From where does their confidence originate? Are their perceptions of Judas and Mary from their education, or is there a created field of collective consciousness embedded with false stories of Judas and Mary that they are tapped into, which then has a corresponding influence on how they think and what they believe?

Have we left ourselves interacting with the fields we have co-created through our collective thinking? How are we affecting these fields, and in turn, how are these fields affecting us? If we collectively built energetic fields of prostitute and betrayer, what is coming back to us? Is it a closed circuit? Are we keeping ourselves imprisoned with our collective thinking? Are these fields extensive that when the next generation comes alone, it is easier for them to tap into that field through entrainment as well as feed it through believing in it and therefore expanding it? Suppose a significant portion of humanity, for centuries, has contributed to the false fields of Jesus, Judas, and Mary. In that case, I can imagine that the fields we have co-created could use some healing.

If a created field of consciousness is based on a distorted view of Jesus, could it influence people to do harmful things in the name of Jesus and feel justified? If so, can this field be weakened or even entirely dismantled with love and truth? Perhaps there has been a constructed field of Judas laden with a grand distortion of who he truly is. There has been much anti-Semitic sentiment and violence done in the name of Judas. Who else's name has been used to justify such extreme darkness?

I wonder if humanity has created distorted fields of consciousness, and then over time, the fields have taken on a life of their own and evolved into a form of false gods. What happens when millions of people over thousands of years continue to feed these distorted fields of consciousness? If we praise a false god or believe a distorted view of Jesus, does our praise turn into energy that feeds the distorted field? Perhaps through rituals, symbols, images, the written word, sermons, and speeches, we enhance the entrainment to a particular field. If we practice rituals born from a distorted level of consciousness, I imagine the ritual would lead us further away from our truth rather than towards our truth.

It is fascinating to contemplate the use of stories as it relates to fields of consciousness. Mary Magdalene's story was rewritten into that of a prostitute and then perpetuated for over 1300 years afterward. Many people have fueled this story by writing books about this untruth as if it was a fact. It is profoundly ironic that Mary's false account of being a prostitute has been used in a way to help and inspire; if Mary can be loved by Jesus, so can we, and if Mary can turn herself around, so can we. If the foundation of the story is a lie, how can it truly bring freedom? Judas's account has not only been perpetuated; it has gotten much worse as he has been increasingly villainized over the centuries (as further discussed in Part 3).

It seems like the fields of consciousness that hold the stories of Judas and Mary have expanded and taken on lives of their own. When people tap into these fields, are they, in turn, placed under the spells of these stories? By spell, I don't mean witchcraft, but the spell cast by the written word being spelled out into false reports. It leads me to wonder if we can be hypnotized by a field of consciousness that we ourselves created. Are we trapping ourselves within our own creations?

Where did fabricated stories of Judas and Mary originate? Some speculate that religious leaders were determined to control people; thus, they intentionally used stories to establish conformity and manipulate thinking and behavior. However, I wonder what was influencing the leaders; was the field of consciousness they were tapped into intentionally steering them away from certain truths? Did they distort the truth because the field of consciousness they tapped into was a field of distortion? Did people innocently and unaware create fields of consciousness related to Judas and Mary that spiraled out of control? What level of consciousness influenced the initial writers of the stories of Judas and Mary; what was dictating their thoughts and behaviors as they dictated fabricated stories? What if their accounts are nothing but manufactured facts from distorted fields that we bought into and believed to be true?

I have thought that human behavior and beliefs could be mainly understood through sociology and psychology; we get indoctrinated and socialized into a way of being, believing, and behaving. That alone can explain how we can become a product of the environment and social, political, educational structures in which we were raised. Yet, I wonder what is influencing those structures. What is the ultimate causal point of the structures, and what are the energetics behind the systems themselves?

By placing a curse on Judas, did we curse ourselves? Did we create a feedback loop of betraying and prostituting ourselves? Are we betraying our true selves and selling /

prostituting ourselves to the matrix, holding ourselves in thought prisons? Are Judas and Mary holding a truth that we suppressed by our collective thinking of them? Can they help us dismantle the corrupt fields and guide us to align to the truth that has been hidden in them as a so-called prostitute and a so-called betrayer?

While pondering about Judas, the medicine he holds, I wondered if part of Judas's Divine mission is linked to helping us break free of all types of false gods that we may be worshiping / fields of consciousness we are entrained to which conditioned us to look outside ourselves for truth; to support us in our knowing and help us to discern truth via our hearts. In a previous journey, I briefly saw Judas as a king and in a future journey as a divine being heading towards the higher realms of heaven. Is Judas guiding souls out of the closed system of the fabricated Earth and false heaven and towards the beam of white light that reaches up the True Heavens and eternal life? If Judas broke out of the consciousness of hell, perhaps he can lead us in breaking out of anything.

If false gods, matrices, and constructed fields of consciousness are at play, then how do we discern truth from illusion? How do we step outside the confines of a conditioned reality and into an awareness that is untainted by centuries of manipulation? It seems that the key lies in developing a refined awareness, a capacity to perceive beyond the limitations of inherited narratives and entrained thought patterns. Perhaps the ultimate gnosis is not merely about acquiring knowledge but about attuning ourselves to a vibrational alignment with the highest truth.

This brings me back to my original question: What is a false god? Could it be more than just an entity or an idea—it could be a frequency, a distortion in the fabric of consciousness that leads us away from our divine nature? If so, then our liberation might not be about escaping a physical realm but about shifting our vibrational state, dissolving the layers of deception, and reclaiming the essence of who we truly are.

In the end, perhaps the only way to truly navigate these questions is not through belief, but through direct experience. To become conscious of the unseen forces shaping our reality, to witness how our thoughts and emotions interact with energetic fields, and to cultivate a state of awareness that allows us to perceive beyond the veil. Could it be that our awakening is not about defeating an external oppressor but about removing the blindfolds we have placed upon ourselves?

Judas Christ is Born

In this journey, I was Judas's mother. Spirit guided me to facilitate a healing and an initiation for Judas. As his mother, I was led to an altar where I was to stand on Judas's behalf. Judas was not prepared for the initiation to come, and until he was ready, I was to stand in his place at the altar. I held space for him, as a proud mama, until he was prepared.

When he joined me, I stepped back from the altar. He was strong enough to do the process on his own. From a distance, I supported him. At one point in the healing, I noticed that Judas had three heads, and he was trying to sort out the different ones. I let Judas know I gave birth to a being that had only one head. He claimed his proper head and discarded the others, which represented false stories and archetypes about him.

Judas stood at the altar and continued claiming his true self. Judas went through an initiation that transformed his being. He was no longer a man working to figure out his truth, nor someone who was struggling to integrate his fragments. After his initiation, Judas stood in alignment with the True God and Jesus and was part of a healed brotherhood. Judas became a king and took a seat at the head of the ceremonial space. I heard Judas claim, "I am Judas Christ." When this announcement was made, it felt like an enormous pronouncement that echoed through time and space: Judas Christ has been born.

<u>Contemplations:</u>

It is significant to me that his mother, in a previous journey, claimed her Christed-self and then helped Judas do the same. His mother went through the process first, then was able to hold space for her son. Judas's mother played an instrumental role in Judas's healing process. In a previous journey, she held space for him in the darkness of hell as he cleaned up his cell. Here, she supported Judas in finding his truth. Judas's mother held potent and powerful medicine for Judas, the medicine of love and belief in her child. When she declared that she gave birth to a son with only one head, it felt like her words carried the medicine of truth that helped Judas discard false stories and archetypes about him. I wonder if one of the extra heads represented the archetype of the betrayer, and the other represented the false story of his death.

In the *Gospel of Judas*, Jesus calls Judas the 13th daimon / god, and says that he will become the ruler of the 13th Aeon. According to gnostic literature, the 13th Aeon is the highest level of heaven in this universe. I wonder if the 13th daimon correlates with the notion of "brotherhood" which is introduced here and then again in future journeys.

The 13th Aeon is the highest realm within this universe, often associated with divine knowledge, transcendence, and liberation from lower material constraints. The Great White Brotherhood is a mystical concept found in Theosophy and various esoteric traditions. It refers to an assembly of enlightened beings or ascended masters who guide humanity's spiritual evolution. The 13th Aeon, being the highest level within this universe, would place Judas in a position of enlightenment, perhaps among those who guide human souls toward liberation.

The number 13 is often associated with death and rebirth, transformation, and initiation into higher wisdom. In esoteric traditions, it represents the passage beyond illusion into true understanding. The Great White Brotherhood is said to consist of beings who have undergone such transformation—so if Judas attained the 13th Aeon, he could be seen as undergoing a similar initiatory process.

The Gnostic idea of liberation from the material world aligns with the Brotherhood's mission of guiding souls toward higher consciousness. If Judas, as the 13th god, was assigned to rule the highest Aeon, it suggests he had reached the pinnacle of understanding—much like the spiritual adepts of the Great White Brotherhood.

If Judas was a chosen vessel for divine knowledge, could the vilification of Judas have been a distortion meant to obscure his true role? Many esoteric traditions suggest that figures who carried deep wisdom were later demonized or erased from mainstream religious narratives. Perhaps Judas, rather than being cast into darkness, was actually being prepared to ascend into divine service—similar to the way the Brotherhood is said to assist humanity.

Moving Statues

I saw a gigantic statue of Jesus, the one in Brazil called Christ the Redeemer. Right next to it was a same sized statue of Judas. The statues were able to move their arms and were holding hands.

<u>Contemplations</u>:

Judas and Jesus appearing as statues felt significant to me as statues are solid, grounded, and not easily moved; statures are well anchored on Earth. It felt significant that out of all the statues that could have appeared in my visions, I saw the biggest one I am aware of, Christ the Redeemer. I wonder if the massive size represented the enormous impact of both Jesus and Judas on the world. These statues were well-grounded, and at the same time, they had movement within their arms. This movement allowed for Jesus and Judas to be holding hands. The holding of hands felt like they were connected in their mission.

I Am Judas - I Am Mother

In this journey, I traveled well beyond this plane of existence. It was beautiful and bewildering all in one. As the journey began, my thoughts became rhythmic as if they were a part of the heartbeat of the universe. One thought led to another, and all thoughts were connected to all other thoughts. The rhythm in the words was connected through sound waves and extended into infinite nothingness. Everything felt connected within one giant web.

As the journey continued, it began to feel like space and time were collapsing. The collapsing felt like the very last moments of our existence on Earth. I thought everyone and this entire existence was dissolving into nothingness. I became aware of two planets: the Earth where we are all living and a New Earth that was in the process of being born. The current Earth was not morphing into the New Earth; it was dissolving into nothingness. The New Earth was being born from a funnel shape made out of space-time fabric. I thought this was the end and the beginning.

I looked up at the sky and saw the stars falling towards the Earth. It was not a meteor shower as the stars were not jetting across the sky horizontally but falling vertically in masses. It was beautiful.

Then I was both 'The Mother' and Judas. As The Mother, it was time to take my seat. As The Mother, I was also Grandmother. As Mother and Grandmother, I was supposed to face a group of people and tell them who I was as Judas. I was to share the story, the whole story. As The Mother, I was to birth the story. As the journey continued, everyone knew the entire story through a connected consciousness. I didn't have to verbalize the story because everyone knew. I was relieved I didn't have to narrate the story as that felt like an enormous responsibility.

I would feel my Kerry-ness from time to time, and as I did, I felt so confused about being 'The Mother', let alone Grandmother. How on Earth was I The Mother? How could it be remotely possible that I was to birth anything as the female elder? I was utterly mystified and perplexed by this notion.

Then, as the Mother / Grandmother, I was to walk up to a male elder and match him and, in doing so, balance the masculine and feminine. I started my journey towards him. I approached an altar and gained my strength. I then walked with the power of a tiger. As I continued walking towards this male elder, he stood up from his seat and departed the area. It was my time as The Mother, and I was to dance the dance of The Mother. I danced in front of the group, and when I finished dancing, I sat in the elder's seat. There was a new consciousness being born that was replacing the old.

I left the elder's seat. I looked back and noticed that the seat was empty. I was elated! No one was sitting there. Not male, not female, as this was not about the feminine taking the seat of the masculine, but about balance. Looking at the empty seat brought much joy. There was no more patriarchy or matriarchy, but a kind of 'uniarchy' that combined them both.

Then I screamed. I screamed for nothingness and everything. This Earth was again dissolving into nothingness, and a New Earth was being born. Sound, the origin of everything, felt very appropriate and necessary, even if it was in the form of a scream. I was screaming to birth the New Earth, break through boundaries, cross thresholds, and shatter with sound, the old story of Judas.

Then I was Judas. I was not a betrayer but part of the healed brotherhood. I was not incarcerated in hell but incarnated back to Earth. The knowing that the scriptures were wrong was apparent. The knowing was in the very fiber of the universe. The story The Mother was to tell, and that everyone knew through the connected consciousness was that Judas didn't betray Jesus, he was killed, and he is a king, a savior, and Christified.

As I was Judas, I searched for Jesus. I was looking for his physical presence in his human body. At first, I couldn't find Jesus. I continued looking for Jesus in a physical form and wondered where he was. "Where is Jesus?" I asked myself over and over. Then I knew Jesus was everywhere. I still could not see him in a physical form, but I could feel his essence permeating everything.

Then, I was the extremes, and I was nothing. I was Mother and Judas at the same time, and somehow that made perfect sense. Both The Mother and Judas were birthing a new consciousness, manifesting a new reality. The Mother was giving birth to the New Earth. Judas was birthing a consciousness. Judas's 'delivering' Jesus to the authorities was seen as the labor and the delivery, not of a baby, but the Christ Consciousness. At this moment, Judas was a mother.

Then, an enormous infinity symbol blossomed out of my heart area. On one side, I was Mother; on the other side, I was Judas. I was both Mother and Judas, both male and female. Then I became the infinity symbol. Enormous energies moved from one side of the symbol through the center to the other side. I was stationary in the middle. In the extremes, there were no more extremes. Duality was collapsing onto itself. It was the beginning and the end. I was everything and nothing. I was mystified and bewildered, and at the same time, I understood.

Contemplations:

Traveling so far into a space of nothingness and then returning to this 3rd-dimensional reality was not easy. Reentering this time and space was jarring, confusing, and disorienting. It was difficult to comprehend my experience. In the journey, it felt like this world was dissolving and everyone along with it. I was surprised that the final moments were arriving, yet there was not a sense of sadness but an acceptance of the completion of our time.

In this journey, I was relieved that I didn't have to share 'the story.' I remember the anxiety that was building along with the knowing that I was supposed to share. Yet, as the journey continued, I traveled to a place / dimension that no story needed to be told, a place beyond story. In this journey, it felt like this very book, this story of Judas that I am writing now, existed in the space-time continuum as a form of consciousness.

At the time of this experience, I did not know what the gnostic texts contained; I only knew they existed. Interestingly enough, the gnostic texts mention three aspects of my journey: this Earth dissolving; stars falling; and the merging of male and female. In the *Gospel of Mary*, there is a similar vision of the world dissolving. The Earth was not evolving into a new creation but towards a process of dissolving into emptiness, identical to my journey.

In the *Gospel of Judas*, when Jesus teaches the mysteries of creation, he mentions that the false creator god, Saklas, will complete "the span of time assigned for him." There was an allotted amount of time that the false gods were to rule over this material world. When the end time comes, what the false god created will collapse. In the end, the True God reclaims its power over creation, and the lower gods will be destroyed, along with their stars. In gnostic texts, falling stars indicate a time of completion and the end of the false gods' reign.

Within the notion of as above, so below, is there something we can tangibly experience as it relates to the notion of true and false gods, the dissolving of the world as we know it, and the falling of stars? If it is true that the false gods of the heavens had an allotted amount of time to rule and they are falling, are we seeing the corresponding fall of the gurus on the earth plane? Within the principle of as above so below, perhaps the two cannot be separated. Those we have viewed as 'stars' in our world of spirituality have been under increased scrutiny in the last few years. The shadow side that exists within some spiritual communities is being revealed at an accelerated rate. Is the fall of the heavenly stars related to the fall of the gurus we see worldwide?

Before this journey, I considered our evolution as moving from one dimension to another and had never thought about the possibility of the Earth dissolving. In this journey, I was confused that this Earth was dissolving, and a new, separate Earth was being born. This was not a process of evolution from one dimension to another as the current Earth was not evolving into the New Earth. The New Earth was being born out of the fabric of spacetime. This did not feel like a snake shedding its skin where there is a continuation of its essence as it evolves and transforms. This was akin to the snake disappearing and a new snake emerging from the fabric of space-time.

Another component of my journey that resembled teachings in gnostic literature was the combination of male and female. The *Gospel of Thomas* and other gnostic teachings touch upon the notion of being both male and female. In my case, both Judas and 'The Mother.' In the *Gospel of Thomas,* passage 22 reads:

> *Jesus said to them, "When you make the two one, and when you make the inside like the outside and the outside like the inside, and the above like the below, and when you make the male and the female one and the same, so that the male not be male nor the female; and when you fashion eyes in the place of an eye, and a hand in place of a hand, and a foot in place of a foot, and a likeness in place of a likeness; then will you enter the kingdom." (Thomas 22).*

What does it mean to make male and female into a single one? The gnostic myth provides some framework for an explanation. To me, myths do not provide facts but provide concepts to ponder, which support us in understanding the incomprehensible. From one gnostic view, humans were created whole and in a spiritualized body. Eating from the Tree of Life brought a 'death' of our wholeness as we split into Adam and Eve. Some Gnostics consider this split from unity, a separation from our divinity, not a division of masculine and feminine related to gender. Adam represents our divinity, and Eve represents our humanity. Therefore, one interpretation of our creation is not based on creating male and female human beings, but two selves: angelic selves (male) and human selves (female). Humans are all female elements, and we exist in a kind of alienation from our higher, masculine, angelic selves. The separation of Eve from Adam represents this alienation. Therefore, salvation is the female element's return to the male element; Eve being reincorporated into Adam (Brakke, 2015).

When reflecting upon my journey through the lens of gnostic teachings, I wonder if being both Judas and Mother / Grandmother was about this merging of the two selves, making male and female into a single one. Was this merging what brought forth the infinity symbol where I sensed unity by experiencing all of duality? It was beyond extraordinary. Feeling connected to everything through nothingness was astonishing. In that space, everything made sense; there were no questions, just an experience of being. The incomprehensible was manageable, such as: being both Judas and 'The Mother' simultaneously; the notion of Judas as a mother; and even Earth dissolving. This feeling of expansiveness, nothingness, and perception originated from the balance and inclusiveness of duality.

Entering the Heavenly Realms

I was Judas's mother. I was on Earth, and Judas was among the Archangels, including Michael. Archangel Michael provided Judas with angel wings and a throne and assisted Judas with heavenly matters. I saw Judas flying around with wings, and I felt so proud of him, as any mama would. I thought to myself, "Wow, that is my son. He owns and wields his powers." He kept on flying higher and higher towards the heavens. As he did, the feeling I had of being proud was then blended with a profound loss. Judas had been resurrected, which was beautiful, and yet, the loss of his physical presence was excruciating. I was mournful, though I knew the transition was good.

Then, I was no longer his mother. I saw Judas with his mother in a church. This church was in a different realm, one I could not reach but could catch a glimpse of from a distance. It was the most beautiful church I had ever seen. Judas and his mother walked down the center aisle of the church. There was an immensely beautiful ceremony being held for him. I was joyful and yet so deeply saddened. Though I was happy for Judas and his mother, I honestly felt such a profound loss, an unexplainable sadness to see them together. My job felt complete.

Judas was then far within the heavenly realms, a place I could not go. As he journeyed further, he was no longer in human form. He was a bright, white radiance of light. As he traveled, an explosion of white light occurred in the heavens.

I see a bed of eternal rest being presented to me. It is golden and in a heavenly space. I rest.

Contemplations:

Judas had been working towards being grounded on this earth plane, and then, in this journey, he departed to the heavens. It felt appropriate that his mother would be the one walking him down the aisle as mothers bring forth birth and delivery. This felt like the delivery of Judas to another realm yet, where were they going? In the *Gospel of Judas*, Judas was to rule over the 13th Aeon, the highest level of heaven in this universe. Was his mother walking him to this heaven? Did his essence transition into a bright, white radiance of light because he was done with his human journey? What was the explosion of white light in the heavens? It was magnificent, yet I could only sense a feeling of celebration, unification, and completion and felt there was much more to this explosion.

Judas entering the high reaches of heaven with a corresponding explosion of white light reminds me of a passage in the *Gospel of Judas*. In the passage, Jesus instructs Judas to gaze upon a cloud. *"Judas lifted up his eyes and saw the luminous cloud, and he entered it"* (Judas 57). As Judas enters the cloud, he sees his future of transcending the material world and returning to his heavenly home. Is this passage, along with what I saw in my journeys, a description of Judas's transfiguration?

There was much I was not privy to in this journey, and I saw several images from a distance. I was not privy to what happened in the heavens with Archangel Michael, what happened with his mother in the church, nor within the heavenly realms that Judas entered. There was magnificence and a mystery all in one.

Deep sadness arose when I was weeping after Judas ascended as well as when I saw him with his birth mother. For over a year, the sadness I felt would return by merely thinking about this particular journey. I can't explain why I felt such a loss after my role as his mother was complete. The completion of my role as his mother ached in my heart.

The overlap between information in the *Gospel of Judas* and my visions truly stunned me. I was surprised to see a correlation between my journeys and this ancient gnostic text when I had not even read it or even knew it existed at the time of my visions. While some information confirmed my visions, other passages in the gospel helped me understand my journeys. There is much more to the gospel than what I delve into in this book. The parts of the gospel that coincides with my journeys include:
- the notion of a true and false god, two heavenly realms, and two kinds of humans;
- falling stars;
- Judas didn't commit suicide, he was stoned to death;
- the curse and being persecuted by others; and
- Judas being not only a good guy but a divine being that transcended the material world and returned to his heavenly home.

I am happy that I did not know about the gospel before my journey with Judas, as I would have believed that what I read infiltrated my consciousness and shaped my journeys and visions.

Embodying Judas

Spirit asked me to embody the essence of Judas, to embody all of him, including his wings. To do this, I had to head to an altar in the center of the ceremonial space. I walked towards the altar and collapsed onto the floor as I felt the intensity of this process well before I reached the altar. I rested on the floor until I built up the strength to slowly make it the rest of the way. After I arrived at the altar, I rested beside it until I was ready.

I rested until I had the capacity to stand as Judas. It took much strength and time to do this. I would try and then be back on the floor. I got to my feet and trembled with my hands on my knees. I stood up and shook. To extend his wings took great effort. I embodied Judas. I showed Judas on this earth plane for all those who were meant to see him.

I left the altar and rested. I rested until I, still embodying Judas's essence, was asked to return to the altar to receive Jesus. I walked back to the center of the ceremonial space and stood on one side of the altar. Jesus was on the other side. Judas faced Jesus and received him. As Roc-a-Sha, I felt like a fulcrum through which Jesus and Judas were merging.

<u>Contemplations:</u>

Spirit asked me to embody the purest form of Judas I could. I had held a fragment of him, a broken part of him. Now I was being asked to embody as much of his pure essence as I could. I could barely do this. I know I only incorporated what I could, and even that was challenging. It was significant that this process didn't happen until after Judas had ascended into the heavens as I was not being asked to show anything but the purest form of him. What did it mean to embody Judas for all those who were meant to see him on the earth plane? Why was I even necessary? What would his essence bring coming through me, rather than just appearing on his own?

What agreement did I make with Judas? Did it entail carrying a fragment, offering support in his healing process, working with his mother, and writing a book? What about this moment of embodying Judas for all who were meant to see him, and then fusing with the essence of Jesus? Was this all part of the agreement from the beginning? I wonder how I can best understand and embrace all aspects of my connection to Judas.

A merge of Judas, Jesus, and myself happened when I was given my name Roc-a-Sha, and then again in this journey. What did it signify that the essence of Judas and the essence of Jesus merged? Were Judas and Jesus a part of the same consciousness, then separated, and now coming back together?

A Tear in the Universe

I saw Jesus and Judas, in their sacred union, sewing a tear in the universe. It was through this tear that evil had been born. After some time passed, the universal wound healed, and Judas and Jesus removed the stitches. In this process, Jesus and Judas were not only healing this tear but also anchoring unity into Earth and restoring "the brotherhood."

Contemplations:

In previous journeys, Judas and Jesus merged. In this journey, they were united yet remained individuals. I wonder if Judas and Jesus are part of the same consciousness. Were they separated / divided, and now since they are united / merged, can anchor unity and restore the brotherhood? What is the significance of this brotherhood that has emerged in different journeys? Who made up the brotherhood? What happened to the brotherhood that it even needed to be restored? Can the brotherhood be mirroring unification and the experience of oneness?

In Theosophy, and various mystical traditions, The Great White Brotherhood is a group of highly evolved spiritual beings, ascended masters, and enlightened teachers who guide humanity's evolution. These beings are said to have transcended the cycle of reincarnation and now assist in raising human consciousness. Often associated with figures like Jesus, Buddha, Saint Germain, and Kuthumi, the Brotherhood is not a formal organization but a spiritual hierarchy working beyond the physical plane.

If we consider Judas in the context of the Great White Brotherhood, several intriguing possibilities emerge. One key idea in Theosophy and esoteric teachings is that some souls willingly take on difficult or misunderstood roles in service of a greater divine plan. Rather than being a fallen disciple, could Judas have been an advanced initiate within the Brotherhood?

In this journey, Judas and Jesus were sewing a tear in the universe. It was through this tear that evil had been born.

I wonder if the gnostic gospels refer to this tear with different terms. In the *Gospel of Judas,* Jesus teaches Judas about the structure of the universe, including the difference between the True God and the false gods. Jesus explains how there is a powerful and all-loving God, and yet there is evil, injustice, and suffering in this world because the false gods created it. The false gods are mortals with an incomplete understanding of divinity and possess limited skills. They are flawed, and their creations are flawed. Did the false gods separate / tear away from the True God? Was this separation from the True God, the tear through which evil was born?

In gnostic thought, the True God is beyond form, beyond duality, while the false gods operate within limitation and control. If the false gods represent a separation from the divine fullness (pleroma), then the act of Judas and Jesus mending the tear could symbolize the reintegration of divine wisdom into our fractured reality.

If the brotherhood being restored mirrors unification, then it suggests that separation—whether between Judas and Jesus, humanity and divinity, or individuals within themselves—is an illusion. The brotherhood's restoration is not just about a spiritual group but about reestablishing a cosmic principle: the experience of oneness that transcends division.

Witnessing the Glory, Not the Story

In this journey, I married Judas. This was not a romantic marriage, yet the word marriage was used. I went to an altar for the marriage ceremony.

The medicine of being married involved witnessing the glory, not the story, in others. Spirit explained that we all have our life experiences, yet we are not our life experiences. The ins and outs of being human were about being in and then out of form; about being in our stories, and then knowing we are not our stories. Yet, while not being our stories, they can be vehicles to expansiveness if used correctly. Deeply processing our stories, fully embracing all of our existence can lead us into restoration.

Judas and I teamed up to offer healings to others. We had separate jobs that united us as a team. I was to witness the person as healed, and Judas did the healing. I witnessed the glory, and Judas entered 'the story.' My attention was to remain on their perfection, witness their soul and the individual's glory.

<u>Contemplations</u>:

In this journey, I did not merge with Judas but married him. The merging in past journeys felt like our individual essences being absorbed into one; two combined spirits in one body. Being married, Judas and I remained as separate individuals and had our distinct roles. Working with Judas felt magical as his healing medicine embraced witnessing someone's glory while in human form. Judas was present to the most challenging part of someone's story and supported them in excavating their deepest wounds. My role of witnessing people in their perfection reminded me of an earlier journey when Judas was integrating his fragments, and my purpose was to see Judas as already healed.

There was an understanding of not being our stories but not avoiding them either. Just because our spirits transcend our stories, our experiences are not to be dismissed while in form. There is medicine in processing our stories as bypassing our pain does not bring glory. While not being attached to our stories, there was an understanding to be present with them. Being present with our stories allows us to deconstruct them and be more fully alive while in the physical.

I wonder if the marriage of Judas and me relates to the gnostic teaching of joining our male and female, human and divine selves. Did teaming up with Judas provide a glimpse of what this would feel like if I was wholly joined / married to my divine self? When these two parts are married entirely, what is our experience?

Ark of the Covenant

I heard the questions from Spirit, "Will you write the book? Will you write the story of Judas? Will you write the truth?" I accepted without hesitation. After agreeing, I was told that the truth of Judas resides in the Ark of the Covenant. His story lives there. When I was told his story lives in the Ark, there was an emphasis on the word 'lives' in the present tense. This was not a dead history or a story of the past, but an active and an alive account. I was told that his story lives in the Ark and that the Ark is in the center of the Earth.

Contemplations:

At the time of this vision, I was so excited to write this book. During this series of journeys, much felt magical and wondrous, and I experienced much joy. Now, putting this on paper feels daunting and complex at times. Though I agreed to write 'the truth,' I acknowledge that it does not mean that I have written Judas's absolute truth. It only means that I am doing my best to understand and articulate the complexity and multidimensionality of my experience. All I can offer is a book of mystery with literally over 400 question marks. I pray this book does justice to what Spirit and Judas have asked of me.

I wonder what it means that Judas's story lives in the Ark of the Covenant and that the Ark is in the center of the Earth. Perhaps it indicates his story, with all else in the Ark, is central to our existence on Earth? Though I cannot imagine the actual Ark in the center of the planet, the Ark's essence could very well reside there in a higher vibrational state. Some consider the center of our Earth molten; others have a hollow Earth theory. I now have a Hallow earth theory.

The time-lapse I saw at the end of this journey added to a previous one. The time-lapse sequences provided a recap. Judas was once in the consciousness of hell and now in the Ark of the Covenant. It reminds me of the infinity symbol, with each side holding an extreme and the middle point being that of neutrality. From hell to the Ark, what does all this mean?

Five White Petals

Spring had arrived, and the stone fruits like plum and cherry trees were blossoming. The blossoms were made of five white petals. The flowers were growing in clusters of three to five flowers.

There was an emphasis on the number three evolving into the number five: the trinity of the Father, Son, and Holy Spirit joined with Judas and The Divine Mother.

<u>Contemplations:</u>

A trinity was present in previous journeys where, on several occasions, I was asked to make a triangle with my two thumbs and two pointer fingers connected. Spirit guided me to look into the triangle. Deep in the triangle was Jesus as well as an entire universe. Inside the triangle was always beautiful and expansive, which evoked a deep sense of boundlessness. This boundlessness was the specific medicine that the triangle held. I was encouraged to use this medicine and work with the symbol of the triangle. Sometimes I would be a part of the trinity of points symbolizing Judas, Jesus, and myself. The triangle felt like a symbol of Roc-a-Sha, where the three of us were united in one.

In this journey, the trinity appeared as the Father, the Son, and the Holy Spirit. The trinity was evolving to include the Divine Mother and Judas. The fruit trees held not only the symbolism of five petals but also the symbolism of fruit. This was not just a spring of rebirth, but the birth of a new fruit, the fruit of five. The five embodies the consciousness of a pentad: *Father, Son, Holy Spirit, Judas, and the Divine Mother.*

Within the context of the number five, it is fascinating to contemplate the 5-pointed star. This one star has many meanings spanning from representing the devil to being used in ancient times as a Christian symbol for the five wounds of Christ. When the star is right side up, it is seen as a symbol of light; when it is upside down, it is seen through a dark lens. Just as the 5-pointed star has been seen through both the lens of light and dark, so has Judas.

Interestingly, the upside-down star fits perfectly inside the star that is right-side up, and then an upright star fits into the upside-down star, and so on into infinity (see the star above). The star perfectly fits the darkness inside the light, then the light inside the dark into infinity. This reminds me of the merging of the duality that leads to a sense of nothingness and expansiveness that I felt with the experience of the infinity symbol.

Judas and Magdalene

I felt Judas entering into my heart, and as he did, I sensed he was assisting Mary Magdalene. I was deeply confused on why Mary would need healing, as well as why this would happen in my heart. I remained aware that healing was occurring but was not privy to the details of what was unfolding.

<u>Contemplations</u>:

I found it difficult to grasp the idea that Mary needed healing. I was not aware of how or with what Judas was assisting her. I wonder if Mary's healing journey was similar to Judas's, given that both have been misrepresented and subjected to false narratives. For centuries, massive untruths have been cast upon them, and I question how this has influenced their very essence as well as the fields of consciousness connected to them.

Jesus's Love and Judas's Medicine

Judas offered me a healing session. Judas guided me to gather all the unhealed aspects of me that I could at that moment. I was to access the most profound pain I could, incredibly intense shame, guilt, and feelings of being unlovable. Judas instructed me to gather in, not to reject or push away, but to grab ahold of the deepest hurts and fragmented parts of myself and to bring them deep within my heart. This process was about reaching into the darkness and collecting the most hurt parts of myself. It was not about clearing, removing, or transcending, but embracing. It was about saying yes to the darkest parts of me, without denying, trying to escape, or push away.
It was not about fixing but accepting.

While holding an awareness of my deepest hurts, I was to embrace the essence of Judas Christ. I was not Judas, nor married to him, but embodying his medicine and folding into this medicine the pain that I carried. Then I entered a tomb. In this tomb, Judas stood behind me as I faced Jesus. I was to face Jesus's love with the very parts of me that I felt could never be loved. The love of Jesus entered me as I embodied the essence of Judas's medicine. I brought fragmented parts of me that were living in the darkness into the light present in my heart. This light encompassed Jesus's love and Judas's medicine, which together held an uncompromising acceptance of everything. This light held the unbounded consciousness of love and had the capacity to embrace deep hurts.

I was guided to 'activate the Judas Christ' inside of me to transform my pain. I could feel that Judas held 'my story,' which allowed me to experience a glimpse of 'glory.' This glory rested under all the narratives, beliefs, and traumas I have held. This deep rest was the eternal rest I had a glimpse of in a previous journey. This rest was eternal, yet it was up to me to rest in this space. I had the option to venture back to my head and into the stories or rest deep in my heart.

This was a process of death and birth. It was the death of many stories, as well as the heaviness and dread that I once carried. The death and rebirth happened within the light of my heart, where the light was consuming the darkness with the assistance of Judas's medicine and Jesus's love. On the other side of this death was a welcome into a new way of living within the context of all that is; not rejecting, not pushing, not running, but allowing and accepting everything. In this allowance was rest, if I were to choose it.

Contemplations:

The profound beauty of this healing experience feels beyond words. In this healing, there was a merging of Judas, Jesus, and myself, but this time it was Jesus's love and Judas's medicine within my heart. The death and birth process happened within a tomb, which seemed like the most appropriate space for such an experience. It was dark, as tombs can be, but it felt like sacred ground.

Collecting fragments of myself and integrating them within the light of my heart that contained the combination of Jesus's love and Judas's medicine brought a liberation of burdens and a subsequent expansiveness.

Activating the 'Judas Christ' in me as well as Judas standing behind me as I faced Jesus ignited a feeling that anything can be healed, and everything can be loved. This shattered the beliefs I carried most of my life: there are parts of me that cannot be loved, are unworthy of love, and should even remain outside of love. There is nothing that cannot be loved, and there is nothing that needs to remain outside of love. Absolutely everything can be and is loved.

The Medicine of the Middle

I was being shown the number 22. The first two represented duality. The second two represented duality. The two 2s (duality and duality) were canceling out each other. Duality was canceling out duality. Sometimes the number 22 would disappear, and all that was left were 0s and 1s.

These numbers represented the foundational frequencies of creation. The 0s and 1s encouraged the behavior of holding the middle ground and experiencing unity. It was there I found Judas; Judas was holding the middle ground. He was not a villain nor a savior. He was. He was beyond all stories.

I was then shown very dark images and very light images. I felt neutrality towards both. I knew to stay neutral while in the presence of darkness; to not get entangled, engaged, or even react as reacting not only feeds the darkness but can lead one to get entrapped. Then I was shown all sorts of brightly colored objects, and even though they were from the light, I was not attracted to them. I felt neutral to the light as well. I was experiencing neutrality with the dark and neutrality with the light. I felt my breath and remained calm as a ton of energy, colors, and images were presented to me. There was everything and yet nothing to latch onto or embody, all to observe from the observer's perspective. Both the darkness and the light were helping me find my center, the middle ground. This middle ground brought me into my knowing, into alignment, and a 'preparation.'

I saw an enormous infinity symbol made of light emerge from my heart. The center of the symbol was anchored in my heart, and the loops extended out to either side of me. I was guided to focus on the point in the middle, which was in my heart. Information, in the form of light and sound, came in from the right loop and then the left loop. As information reached the middle, it unified multiple worlds. As I focused on the center point, I became all things at once, and then nothing. I was then Grandmother and Judas. At this moment, the central point of infinity, called 'union,' was the disintegration of duality; the dilution of dualities such as the masculine and feminine, good and evil, and heaven and Earth.

At times, there was a massive swirling of energy from one side to the infinity symbol to the other as I anchored in the middle. As the energy moved from one side to another, there was a knowing of individual presences like the Divine Mother being with me. The infinity symbol was encompassing all of what is. If I ever felt unstable within the massive energy movements, Judas helped me anchor in the middle. Judas knew the middle. The middle was the medicine Judas carried. As I journeyed deeper into this space, I experienced:

I am Judas Christ
I am body and Spirit
I am heaven and hell
I am the light and the dark
I am chaos and order
I am fractured and whole
I am remembrance and forgetfulness
I am the betrayer and the betrayed
I am all the stories people have created,
and I am none of those stories
I am suffering and salvation
I am all of creation
I am all of this and none of it
I am Judas Christ

<u>Contemplations:</u>

Though I don't necessarily understand what Spirit was teaching me with the number 22, duality canceling out duality, and the subsequent emergence of unity, I do find it utterly fascinating that the passage in the *Gospel of Thomas* about making the two into one is passage number 22:

> *Jesus said to them, "When you make the two one, and when you make the inside like the outside and the outside like the inside, and the above like the below, and when you make the male and the female one and the same, so that the male not be male nor the female; and when you fashion eyes in the place of an eye, and a hand in place of a hand, and a foot in place of a foot, and a likeness in place of a likeness; then will you enter the kingdom"* (Thomas 22).

The image and experience of the infinity symbol came a few times in journeys. The center of the symbol would be at my heart, and the loops would extend out to either side of me. A massive amount of energy would move through the symbol and bring me into an experience of expansiveness. This experience reminded me of the intense journey where the New Earth was being born. This journey was not about moving from the 3rd dimension to a higher dimension; it was about dissolving into nothingness. It was about being everything and nothing. I was led to enter nothingness through neutrality, and out of the nothing blossomed wholeness.

As the energy swirled through the infinity symbol, it was swirling through all possibilities. Judas Christ was in the middle—both the light and the dark, and in being both, he was also beyond. In Sanskrit, this is echoed in the term neti, neti—not this, not this—a reminder that the core of our Being is beyond all labels and divisions. It is neither this nor that, neither positive nor negative, neither male nor female. It is pure potential, infinite and formless, yet capable of becoming anything. This is the truth of who we are—eternal beings of love—found in that inner space beyond opposition.

Jesus expressed this idea in another way: 'The Son of Man has nowhere to lay His head' (Matthew 8:20). This suggests that true alignment is not found in extremes but in the still point between them. Jesus embodied the middle path, where divine truth transcends polarities. His statement reflects that true rest is not in attachment to worldly divisions but in a deeper, centered alignment. It symbolizes that peace is not found in rigid identification with any one position, ideology, or structure, but in the dynamic equilibrium of divine presence. Jesus' teachings often pointed to an internal kingdom (Luke 17:21), emphasizing that aligning with God requires surrendering extremes and finding peace in the center—where the heart resonates with the divine.

To remain in this center is to dwell in the field of neutrality, a space of pure creative potential that is neither defined nor pulled by external forces. Here, Judas stands—not as a figure of betrayal, but as a presence at the threshold of dissolution and emergence, holding the wholeness that exists beyond duality.

Part 3 – Reflections

The Power of a Story

I am fascinated by the power a story can hold—the stories we have told ourselves, as well as the ones told to us. If a story is used to inspire, it has the ability to infiltrate our being and bring forth change. If an account has been used to persuade, it has the capacity to manipulate us. If we have been lied to and we believe the false story, then that story can hold us in a state of confinement. If we have heard only one side of a story for our lifetime, the other side might feel impossible to be true. Yet, even if a false narrative has endured centuries or thousands of years, it can crumble. I believe that we live in a time where many of us are open to hearing authentic stories of ourselves and the cosmos; truths that update the outdated stories that perhaps we needed to believe until we were ready for the truth. I do feel our cultural narratives are shifting towards having a more solid foundation of truth. The shackles on any trancelike state of cultural story hypnosis are collapsing as we navigate forward in our evolution.

What if the story of Judas fits into this collapse? Some New Testament scholars believe that the story of Judas and the betrayal was fabricated and lacks a historical foundation (Pagels et al., 2008, p. 29). Some have wondered if the authors of the gospels constructed the story of Judas as well as aspects of Jesus's passion, crucifixion, and resurrection by choosing specific passages from the Old Testament prophetic writings (Pagels et al., 2008, p. 27- 29). If so, why would a story be fabricated? If the story was a fabrication, how far were the early Christians willing to go to not only design but also perpetuate a false story, and in doing so creating and maintaining a dominant culture?

I feel we live in a time where many people are open to considering more than what we have been told through history books or holy scriptures, even if it is the complete opposite perspective we are accustomed to. We can have our minds blown; in fact, many long for that. We live in a time of possibility and freedom where falsity can no longer endure as easily, as the grip of untruths is not as steadfast as it once was. The hold that falsities have had on us is loosening as our collective awareness is expanding.

The Gospel of Judas

Something that can help us break any existing shackles of hypnotic, trancelike states created through cultural stories is new information. Yet, sometimes new information is initially rejected by our minds because we cannot comprehend its truth. There can be a process of deep contemplation after we are presented with new constructs as it may require us to dismantle formerly understood notions of reality. New information can come in multiple ways, including scientific understandings, personal meditations, and even lost scriptures.

It was in January of 2019 that I became aware of the *Gospel of Judas*. It had been discovered in the late 1970s by farmers in Middle Egypt near Al Minya. Though the codex containing the gospel was found in the seventies, it wasn't until April 2006 that National Geographic made the *Gospel of Judas* public. In the many years after the discovery and before it was publicly available, the codex containing the gospel was bought and sold by antiquities dealers, traveled across three continents, frozen and thawed, as well as improperly stored for sixteen years in a safety deposit box on Long Island, New York. During this time, the papyrus (a material made from reeds grown along the Nile River) pages suffered much damage and broke down into fragments. The fragments needed to be reassembled for the gospel to be translated from Coptic, the language of the Ancient Egyptians, into English and other languages.

I find it significant that the title given to this Gospel is "The Gospel of Judas." This is not the Gospel according to Judas. Other gospels, such as Matthew, Mark, Luke, and Thomas, are "The Gospel According to..." the author, meaning it is the gospel story of Jesus through the author's lens. There is a significant difference between The Gospel According to Judas and the Gospel about Judas. The *Gospel of Judas* translates as the Good News about Judas and not as the Good News about Jesus as seen through Judas's lens and perspectives (Ehrman, 2006, p. 98).

What is the Good News about Judas? The *Gospel of Judas* portrays Judas as Jesus's closest and most trustworthy disciple, who truly understood who Jesus was and from where he came. Judas was the one and only disciple who received Jesus's teachings of the mysteries of the heavens. In the gospel, the so-called betrayal was not seen as a greedy act nor influenced by the devil, but as a good and necessary act, a request of Jesus that Judas could fulfill faithfully as part of the Divine plan. Because of this act, Jesus tells Judas that he will exceed all the other disciples.

Not only that, but Judas's deed initiates a new cosmic order in which this world ends, and all who follow Jesus will return to their true heavenly home. That is quite an accomplishment and good news!

The *Gospel of Judas* offers a different perspective than the one handed down through the New Testament Gospels of Mathew, Mark, Luke, and John. What does the mind do with new information on Judas presented in the *Gospel of Judas*? Does the mind twist the text to fit the old constructs, or does the mind open to contemplation, which allows for a new perspective? I wonder if I did not have my personal experience with Judas, would I have dismissed the gospel? Would my Catholic upbringing and conditioning prevent my mind from accepting such an alternative view?

I grew up being told that Bible passages were handed down from God to humans. Since the Bible was a God-given book, there was no need to question its origin or content. If I had questions, they could never be about the source of the Bible, only my inability to understand. It was permissible that my intelligence and comprehension were in question, but never the Bible. While in grade school, I had no idea that many writings were sort through in early Christianity, and only select ones made it into the New Testament. I recited the Nicene Creed without knowing that the Roman Emperor Constantine organized a church council at Nicaea in A.D. 325 to diminish opposing views of the competing Christian factions and thereby establishing what was to be considered as orthodox. To create a uniform church, leaders carefully selected which gospels would create the canon while discarding additional texts with nonconforming views.

It was quite the achievement to quiet opposing voices to the point that many people, including myself, didn't even know that there were contradictory ideas about Jesus and the very nature of Christianity. Christianity to me was a uniform, well-structured, clearly laid out system of belief; yet, the early Christian factions were diverse in their cosmology and their understanding of God and Jesus. Early church leaders made a great effort to shape a belief system, a universal church free of controversies over fundamental principles. They freed themselves of disputes over belief by destroying writings, burning buildings, and slandering authors with dissenting views, saying they were dangerous and heretical. Orthodox Christianity emerged after a prolonged fight where church leaders triumphed over dissenting voices. The viewpoint that won was not necessarily the correct understanding, merely the one that gained the most power (Ehrman, 2006, p. 174-175).

The *Gospel of Judas* was written before the Nicene Creed had been established. The author wrote during a time when numerous fractions of Christianity were struggling; people were fighting for their views to be heard and their identity to be recognized. Was the author using the pen to go up against the increasingly influential church leaders who were systematically suppressing opposing voices? The *Gospel of Judas* challenges the very foundation of what became the Orthodox Church. The author writes that Judas was the only one to receive the mystery teachings from Jesus and goes as far as to state that the other disciples who did not receive the teachings from Jesus worshiped a false god. After the deaths of both Jesus and Judas, the only ones left to carry on the teachings were those who didn't know the True God. Since these disciples were said to be the establishment of Christianity, the author asserts the church's foundation is based on the praising of a false god (Pagels et al., 2008, p. 125).

As a gnostic text, the *Gospel of Judas* challenges the notion of how we can come to 'know' God. I was taught that God spoke directly to the authors of the New Testament, and in the present day, God speaks to the Pope, and that information is passed down to cardinals, bishops, deacons, and priests. These men are believed to be the continuous line of the successors of the apostles. Gnostic Christians believed that knowledge of God, Jesus, and Christianity could be revealed to individual Christians outside of the line of successors. An individual can know God directly.

Judas being a traitor is a fundamental 'truth' to many, as it was to me growing up as a child in a parochial school. The *Gospel of Judas* challenges this story of the betrayal. In the *Gospel of Judas*, Judas handed over Jesus to religious authorities to initiate the advent of our ability to know God, the True God, directly. This direct knowledge of the True God would free us from being under the dominion of the false gods who created this world. The betrayal sets in motion the cosmic restructuring necessary for our awakening.

I could not help but wonder what Orthodox Christianity would look like if gnostic texts such as the *Gospel of Judas* were chosen as the biblical canon. What would have been the ripple effect if people were taught how to discern between any false god and the True God; if they knew they could have a direct relationship with the True God without an intercessor like a priest; and if they understood the mysteries of the so-called betrayal as the initiation of a cosmic restructuring?

Historical Judas

There are few sources detailing Judas's life from antiquity that can be considered historically trustworthy. The earliest Christian author, the apostle Paul, made no mention of Judas Iscariot. The earliest mention of Judas occurs in the New Testament gospels, written thirty-five to sixty-five years after his death, in the second half of the first century, possibly between 65 and 95 C.E. In the New Testament, Judas was portrayed as greedy and being eager to betray Jesus for coins (Matthew), as well as influenced by Satan (Luke), and even being the devil himself (John).

Since the gospels were written many years after Jesus's time on earth, they were not written by eyewitnesses but by second- or third-generation Christians. Gospel authors received the stories of Jesus and Judas through oral traditions; they were not necessarily handed down from God as I was taught in grade school. They were also not necessarily written for preserving historical events but to preserve spiritual teachings. As to be expected, their stories align in some cases and conflict in others. I find this to be expected not only because a few generations had passed but also because each author's views, understanding of the stories, and reason for sharing them were individualized and unique.

Within oral traditions, the storytellers were permitted and even expected to alter their stories depending on their audience and reason for sharing. If a particular lesson was to be learned from the story, the story would take a different course. Stories were malleable according to the reason for sharing them. Since reports were shaped and altered to address current times and needs, variations in the stories themselves were expected (Ehrman, 2006, p. 35-36).

This leads me to wonder about the differences in the New Testament Gospels. What were the authors trying to teach through their specific telling of the story of Judas? For example, why would the authors detail the death of Judas and the money he received differently? In Matthew, Judas returned the money he received from the high priests in exchange for betraying Jesus. In turn, the priests bought a field in Jerusalem with the money. After Judas returned the money, he killed himself. In Acts, it states that Judas purchased a piece of land with the money and died not through suicide but by bursting open.

Why are such significant discrepancies portrayed in Matthew and Acts? I can understand the differences in the gospels as they are a product of oral traditions. Yet, I am curious about the morals with the unique variations related to Judas. What lessons were they teaching by claiming Judas was greed-driven or asserting that Satan possessed him? If there was a point in altering the story to teach lessons or make a specific argument, what were those reasons? Were they addressing concerns, trying to use accounts to persuade, to cultivate a particular belief or behavior? Were they trying to shape the consciousness of the culture in which they lived? Were they trying to establish a theological lens? What ultimate purpose did these variations serve?

Over time, Judas's name appeared in additional texts. In the second-century *Papias*, there is mention that Judas "became so bloated in the flesh that he could not pass through a place that was easily wide enough for a wagon—not even his swollen head could fit." The passage continues to state that "his eyelids swelled to such an extent that he could not see the light at all," and when he urinated, "he emitted pus and worms that flowed through his entire body." Later on, in the fifth-century *Arabic Infancy Gospel*, Judas was a devil-influenced childhood friend of Jesus. The text mentions that Satan encouraged young Judas to try and bite Jesus (Meyer, 2007, p. 4). I am curious about the purpose the authors had in sharing such a story. What were the authors attempting to do in the name of Judas?

The literature portraying Judas illustrates a historical progression of him becoming increasingly evil (Meyer, 2007). What influenced this progression? In more recent history, there is mention of Judas in anti-Semitic rhetoric where he has been portrayed as the prototypical Jew who was a greedy, Satan-possessed betrayer who killed Christ. Some feel that the sin of Judas is the sin of all the Jews. To use Judas for anti-Semitic purposes and propaganda without substantial historical evidence of these characteristics is mind-blowing. What sources were they referencing? Were they using a story to manipulate and persuade regardless of accuracy? What leads people to not only fabricate but exaggerate the falsity of Judas to justify genocidal persecution?

The ancient Christian narrative of the so-called betrayal is part of the foundation of the Christian faith. The biblical texts are deemed holy by generations of people, yet this story has been building up to the point that Judas became the symbol of anti-Semitism. How can a sacred text be at the foundation of Judas becoming the epitome of evil, the archetype of deceitfulness, greed, and betrayal if it is not true? Is it because the text itself is not one hundred percent factual that untruths can be manufactured from it? There are so few historical details about Judas. Written proof of his existence independent of the *Gospel of Judas* and the retellings of the New Testament narratives has not been found. We do not know where he was born, who his family was, yet his name and ever-evolving mythology have resounded through history.

The fabrications about Judas far outweigh the historical realities of Judas. With everything that has ever been written about Judas, we still don't have his side of the story. If any facts about the historical Judas were to be discovered, I would imagine them being dismissed by many because the ever-evolving symbolization of Judas as evil has permeated collective consciousness for many generations.

Some people disregard the *Gospel of Judas* as nonsense. I feel the *Gospel of Judas* acts like a sword of truth that cuts through the rhetoric. At a minimum, I believe it provides a pause to check in with what we have taken to be true. The *Gospel of Judas* is not just another version of Judas's story, albeit a very different one. The *Gospel of Judas* provides an alternative portrayal of Judas, deep questioning of the matrix of Christianity and how this matrix has shaped us. Have we been asking the big questions of who we truly are and who God is from within a matrix that not only limits but alters the answers we receive? If we ask a matrix a question, we get a matrix answer. The gospel begets a reexamining of what foundation our questions about life, God, and creation even emerge.

Fabricated, Heretical, and Hidden in the Dark

When early church leaders assembled the Bible, certain gospels were chosen for the canon, while other writings were spoken against, marked as heretical, and even destroyed. I can understand why the *Gospel of Judas* was not included in the canonical texts. It brought a contrasting view of God and even the apostles, which stood in opposition to the kind of church the early leaders intended to create.

Before the formation of the biblical canon, around 180 C.E., the church leader Irenaeus of Lyons summarized the Gnostic gospels in his work *Against Heresies*. In it, he specifically condemned the *Gospel of Judas* as heretical (Pagels et al., 2008, p. xii). Yet, why go to such lengths to denounce it rather than simply dismissing it? Did the *Gospel of Judas* pose a threat to the emerging religious institution? Was Irenaeus defending orthodoxy against a perceived challenge? If the text was insignificant, why not simply discard the material without much consideration? What was so dangerous about its message that it needed to have a shadow cast over it?

It is fascinating to me that Judas's story in the New Testament might be fabricated (Pagels et al., 2008), and the *Gospel of Judas* was deemed heretical by Irenaeus. What a double whammy! Was there a truth so powerful it needed to be both distorted and marked? If Judas himself knew a truth that threatened the structure early church leaders intended to create through a compilation of writings and gospels, then an effective way to hide Judas's message would be to cast him as both heretical (*Gospel of Judas*) and evil (New Testament).

Marking the truth-tellers as heretical or evil is not an uncommon tactic. If leaders of a dominant culture know a particular truth could give the subculture or counterculture power, they can distort the truth, hide it, or make the person telling the truth into someone unbelievable. Regarding Judas, he was cast as a man that Satan possessed and as a greedy villain willing to hand over beloved Jesus for money. Many have considered Judas as a dweller in the deepest level of hell. Judas was not only made into a dark figure, but his story has a historical progression of getting worse through the centuries.

If Judas does indeed hold a powerful truth, it seems possible that by casting Judas as a dark figure, that the truth he sustains was placed intentionally in the dark. It is one thing to hide a gospel in a dark cave in Egypt. It is another to hide a truth within a constructed consciousness of darkness. If there truly is an awareness, a knowing, a revelation, was it intentionally hidden in a place no one would want to look? Who would look for the truth in a dark place (consciousness of hell) or a dark figure (Judas)? One of the best places to hide anything of immense value, including truth, is in the dark. I would venture to say that not many go looking in the dark for a truth, which leaves the dark not only a suitable but perhaps excellent place for hiding anything.

The Power of Myth

Myths are stories used to help us understand what we are unable to comprehend, help us grasp the ungraspable, and provide a framework on how we relate to all that is. Myths are written to serve a purpose within a society, such as attempting to explain the nature of God, the origins of the world, or to answer existential questions: where we came from; our birth and death; our afterlife; and the understanding of good and evil. Myths can become the central and sacred stories of society. They can establish social norms and act as a guide to navigate through our lives. Yet, if myths originate from the collective mind, can they be based on either collective wisdom or distortion? What if the myth used to help us understand and have a context for our existence was incorrect? Does it then provide us with a broken compass with which we navigate?

As we collectively evolve, does our relationship to the use of myth evolve as well? As we grow, perhaps our need for myth decreases as our capacity for knowing and understanding expands. Is it possible that the role of myth may someday become obsolete; that we evolve beyond the use of myth? Maybe as we evolve, we learn to use myth more wisely. Myth has the extraordinary power to shape culture; if we change the myth or the use of myth we change the culture.

One day I reflected upon the power of myth and superstition as well as how truth can be hidden in what is deemed 'dark.' Since I feel that there was a truth hidden with Judas, yet Judas was cast in the dark, I wanted to find an example to illustrate my thoughts. Making truthtellers and influential people into the dark, evil, vile ones is not a new trick. I thought that Friday the 13th would be a perfect analogy of hiding the truth in the so-called dark as well as the power of myths and superstitions. I have understood Friday the 13th as the day of the Goddess. It was a day to celebrate feminine energy and the cycle of creation, death, and rebirth. The number 13 represents the number of moon cycles women have in a year and has been tied to women's empowerment and strength. Yet, Friday the 13th is considered by many to be bad luck.

My understanding was that the bad luck was related to an effort to dampen women's power. I had this vague memory of a story about a man living in the 1400s named Kramer who vilified women healers, demonized feminine energy, and made Friday the 13th an unlucky day. To me, this was an excellent example of hiding truth, power, and strength in what someone deems as corrupt; hiding the power and strength of women under a notion of bad luck.

To understand the link between Kramer and Friday the 13th being bad luck, I searched for information. I could not find a legitimate source related to Kramer making Friday the 13th a day of bad luck. I did find out that Friday the 13th was predominantly related to Judas Iscariot. Ironically, I was attempting to provide an example of what I meant about hiding the truth in the so-called dark and chose an example without even knowing it was linked to Judas and had been for some time.

Judas was considered to be the 13th guest at the Last Supper, held on Maundy Thursday. The next day was Good Friday, the day of Jesus's crucifixion. The link between 13 people at the last supper and the crucifixion being on a

Friday feels a bit like religious folklore to me. Somehow, when Friday and 13 coincide, it is linked to the so-called betrayal. Friday got a bad rap not only because Jesus was apparently crucified on a Friday, but Cain killed his brother, Abel, and Eve gave Adam the fateful apple from the Tree of Knowledge. On a side note, related to myth and the power of storytelling, there is no mention of an apple in the book of Genesis. Yet, many have been conditioned to believe so through storytelling.

The unluckiness of 13 has a broader history as well. Two events that seem relevant are Loki and the Knights Templar. In ancient Norse lore, Loki, a mischievous god, was the 13th guest at a dinner in Valhalla. Being the 13th upset the balance of the 12 gods already seated and therefore introduced evil into the world. Some folklore historians link the origin of the Friday the 13th superstition to the Knights Templar, a large, powerful group of devout Christians formed in the 12th century to defend the Holy Land. Hundreds of Knights Templar were arrested and killed on Friday the 13th of October in 1307, at the orders of King Philip IV of France.

Regardless of the origin, the superstition is real to many people. To this day, some consider it unlucky to have 13 people over for dinner because it can lead to a fatal event, while others avoid flying on Friday the 13th or sitting in the 13th row of an airplane. The fear of Friday the 13th and the number 13 are so real to some that the phobias have been given names: paraskevidekatriaphobia (Friday the 13th) and triskaidekaphobia (number 13). Due to these phobias, hotels and hospitals often skip the 13th floor, and some airports omit gate 13.

Whether a gate or a building floor has been renumbered, the 13th still exists; it is simply hidden in plain sight. The 13th floor of a building and the 13th row of an airplane still exist when they are numbered the 14th floor / row.

What is fascinating to me is that many people are reported to be afraid of Friday the 13th and yet do not know why it is an auspicious day. Is it a handed-down phobia that is easily digested by the next generation? What else are we buying into without knowing why? It seems like the story of Judas was handed down from one generation to the next, without many people questioning the validity.

I wonder if the timing of the emergence of the Friday the 13th superstition is relevant. Wikipedia states that it originated in the 1890s, which means this has been around for only eight generations. This does not even begin to reach back to the time of Judas. Is it that the closer we were getting to Judas's truth, the more it is buried in the 'dark'? Is there a significant reason that Judas has been increasingly demonized over time? We haven't believed this since the time of Judas, so why the late 1800s?

The number 13 is not only linked to bad luck; it is also associated with a new consciousness arising within the context of numerology. It is fascinating that the Nag Hammadi texts discovered in Egypt in 1945 were contained in 13 leather-bound volumes. The texts were hidden since the early centuries and recently brought to light.

The Bare Truth; Cross to Bear

To me, the notion of bearing a cross is working with something difficult, and through the work, there is liberation or a resurrection. I feel so many of us have been bearing the cross of truth. The carrying of this cross has been about: shining light on falsities; challenging the very nature of our being; deconstructing the false constructs we believed in; and meeting the makers of the matrix, even if they are a part of us. The Judas Cross is one such cross. Collectively, as we expose and weaken any falsity, we are given the opportunity to open to a new level of consciousness and birth truths in their bare essence. The bare truth is the naked truth; it has all falsities stripped away, its essence is fully exposed, and all that remains is truly sacred.

If we deconstruct the mythology of Judas and excavate the truth, what would be the corresponding impact on those of us who believed in the myth of the betrayal? How has the myth of Judas shaped our understanding of God and Jesus, and what it means to be Christian? What is the ripple effect in our human evolution if we 'betray' our loyalty to the story of the betrayal?

What rests on the accuracy of Judas's story? If there is indeed a more authentic and more accurate story, what would the truth of Judas's story convey to humanity? How do the actual and fabricated stories of Judas bring about either the slavery or liberation of aspects of our human consciousness? What truth is under any falsity, and what power does it hold? Is the truth so powerful that there will continue to be tremendous effort to shadow the truth in the contexts of a heretical work based on a malevolent character?

For me, the Judas Cross extends well beyond Judas. If what I was taught about him as a child is not valid, it has made me wonder what else is not true? What other stories that I've been told, as well as the ones I tell myself, are not accurate? The Judas Cross has been about working through the falsities that I have shaped my life with and allowing me to shine a light on what is trustworthy for me. This does not feel like a burdensome cross to bear. Instead, I dance with this cross. I dance with the possibility of liberation that only a bare and sacred truth can birth.

Thirteenth God

In the *Gospel of Judas,* Jesus referred to Judas as the 13th daimon (God), who is to rule over the highest heaven in this universe, the 13th Aeon. In one passage, Jesus said to Judas, *"You thirteenth spirit, why do you try so hard? But speak up, and I shall bear with you" (Judas 44).* In another passage, it is written:

> Jesus answered and said, *"You will become the thirteenth, and you will be cursed by the other generations—and you will come to rule over them. In the last days they will curse your ascent [47] to the holy [generation]."*

These gospel passages caught my attention as they reminded me of my journeys where I saw Judas moving to the high reaches of heaven well beyond any realm I could enter. I wonder, who is Judas to be this 13th God, a ruler over a high heaven. A few passages in the *Gospel of Judas*

distinguish Judas from the other disciples, not in the traditional way of a demonized traitor, but as extraordinary. In one passage, Jesus challenges his disciples to stand up and face him. They all, except Judas, said they are strong but didn't have the capacity to stand.
Judas alone had this ability.

> *[Let] any one of you who is [strong enough] among human beings bring out the perfect human and stand before my face." They all said, "We have the strength." But their spirits did not dare to stand before [him], except for Judas Iscariot. He was able to stand before him, but he could not look him in the eyes, and he turned his face away. Judas [said] to him, "I know who you are and where you have come from. You are from the immortal realm of Barbēlō. And I am not worthy to utter the name of the one who has sent you." (Judas 35).*

Judas alone can stand in the presence of Jesus because Judas could represent the 'perfect' human being. 'Perfect,' in gnostic literature, is a human who has the inner knowing of their divinity ignited. This implies that Judas has a divine spark within him. Judas stands yet, does not look into Jesus's eyes. Perhaps this is because Judas sensed the True God emanating through Jesus's eyes and, out of respect, stands in his perfection but with grace and humility. Or perhaps Judas has a spark that would make him similar to Jesus, but he needed training on fully embodying the spark before making eye contact with Jesus. Regardless, in the gospel, Judas stands and declares that he knows that Jesus is from another realm. The other 11 disciples misunderstand who Jesus is and which God Jesus came from. Judas knows that Jesus came from the realm of Barbelo, the most superior of all Aeons and spiritual realms, the place where all else originates. Judas is then separated from the 11, and Jesus speaks to him privately about the mysteries of the heavens.

> Jesus said to Judas, *"Step away from the others and I shall tell you the mysteries of the kingdom. It is possible for you to reach it, but you will grieve a great deal. [36] For someone else will replace you, in order that the twelve [disciples] may again come to completion with their god."*

In the *Gospel of Judas*, Jesus reveals only to Judas the mysteries of the kingdom. Judas had presented himself as the only disciple to be worthy of such revelations. The teachings on the structure of the universe are extensive and make up a significant portion of the gospel. Jesus explains to Judas that there is a larger universe beyond the physical world, a glorious divine realm of the spirit. The heavenly realm is filled with countless divine beings, and eternal realms called aeons. Along with a True God, there are also lower or false gods. These lower gods created the physical world of chaos and death.

It seems significant that Judas is both separated from the twelve and replaced by another man, Matthias. In the *Gospel of Judas*, it is written, "For someone else will replace you, in order that the twelve [disciples] may again come to completion with their god." Judas being replaced allowed the twelve apostles to remain linked to twelve rulers of the lower world. These were the rulers whom the twelve disciples worshiped (Pagels et al., 2008, p. 125). Since these rulers were given a specific allotted time to reign, I wonder if it was important that the twelve remain a group of twelve and not become a group of eleven because the reign of the twelve rulers of the lower world was not complete.

After Judas broke free from the twelve, he received the teachings on the nature of the universe from Jesus. Perhaps this signifies that he could not fully understand the teachings while he was still within the consciousness of the twelve lower gods. Was part of Judas's task to break out of this consciousness, separating from any falsity it holds? Was there a truth that he can only contain once he was broken free? Was Judas separating from the twelve the very beginning of Judas being initiated to rule over the 13th Aeon? If Judas is the 13th God, does it mean he surpassed the twelve lower rulers and is no longer under their dominion? By breaking out of the twelve, did Judas provide a path and initiate the birth of sovereignty for the rest of us?

In a world speaking much about oneness and how we are not separate, is it essential to separate from old teachings and structures in order to experience the next level of consciousness available to us? It is interesting to note that in the *Gospel of Mary,* Jesus also separated Mary from the disciples and then taught her the mysteries. In both the *Gospel of Mary* and the *Gospel of Judas*, the revelation is given to the ones we have been taught to least expect to be worthy of sacred knowledge. Yet, in both gospels, the ones who stand outside the group are the ones to receive the revelations.

This brings to mind the beatitude that speaks of those who are persecuted for truth, for theirs is the kingdom of heaven:

> *Blessed are those who are persecuted because of righteousness, for theirs is the kingdom of heaven* (Matthew 5).

Could it be that those most vilified—the ones cast out, demonized, and misunderstood—are the very ones clearing a path toward greater freedom? Are they ushering us beyond the age of illusion into an era of direct knowing? Plato once said, *"No one is more hated than he who speaks the truth."* If Judas is one of history's most reviled figures, perhaps this is all the more reason to reconsider what truths he may carry and the role he might play in our collective evolution.

The Curse

Was Judas so committed to Jesus and his mission that he was not only willing to endure persecution but also willing to be cursed? The *Gospel of Judas* does not explain the curse, its effects, or how long it lasts, though it states that Jesus told Judas that the rest of humanity would curse him, yet one day he will rule over them. Jesus speaks with Judas,

> *"You will become the thirteenth, and you will be cursed by the other generations* (the rest of humanity) *—and you will come to rule over them. In the last days they will curse your ascent [47] to the holy [generation]."*

The angrier people are, the more hateful and forceful their energy. Being cursed by a group of outraged, fuming, and furious people, could have been horrendous. The notion of "the rest of humanity" could mean all humanity living in that moment and all humans to come. If this is so, the energy in the curse could have been enormous.

How, if we tell a false story, put it in writing, and perpetuate it over the years, does this affect a soul? What stories were told after Judas's death that perhaps kept his soul damned as the stories were handed down from one generation to the next and got worse over time? It was placed in writing that the devil entered Judas, and he betrayed Jesus. Is this a form of a written curse for billions to read, simply to reinforce and supply the energy for the curse to be maintained by 'the rest of humanity?'

The Day of the Dead is about remembering someone, so they will never truly die. What if someone is remembered as evil? Does that keep an evil curse in place? What is the impact of a perpetual story being circulated amongst the living about the dead?

Is there any link between Judas being cursed and him being the 13th Daimon? Was the curse an initiation? Did Judas need to be cursed and then break free? Was he meant to be condemned before he was to rule? Was the curse necessary and part of his ascension? Is Judas triumphing over a curse, his resurrection?

In Theosophy, suffering, trials, and even condemnation are often seen as necessary stages in the journey toward enlightenment—a form of spiritual alchemy where the initiate transcends the lower self to attain divine realization; ascension through trials. In esoteric traditions, initiates often undergo severe trials, sometimes even public humiliation or condemnation, as a rite of passage into higher knowledge. If Judas was indeed the 13th daimon, his curse may have been an initiation designed to strip away attachments to worldly identity, forcing him to transcend suffering and step into divine wisdom.

Theosophy teaches that spiritual evolution requires transcending karmic burdens. If Judas was condemned unjustly and bore the weight of humanity's projections, breaking free from that curse would symbolize his liberation from the dense energies of the material world. His journey could mirror the alchemical Great Work, where the "base metal" (his cursed state) is transmuted into spiritual gold (his divine rulership).

In many esoteric teachings, a figure must first "descend" before they can "ascend." Some believe that Jesus himself descended into the underworld before rising. Could Judas have been required to experience the depths of condemnation before he could step into his role in the 13th Aeon?

Theosophy speaks of the Dweller on the Threshold, a powerful force that confronts an initiate with the total weight of their karma before they can pass into higher realms. Judas may have faced this kind of trial—not because he was truly cursed, but because he needed to overcome the illusion of condemnation to ascend.

If Judas was destined to rule the 13th Aeon, then his earthly experience of betrayal, cursing, and rejection may have been his trial by fire—one designed to test his ability to hold divine wisdom without being corrupted by suffering. In this way, the curse may have served to purge him of all that bound him to lower states, much like how some

Theosophical and Gnostic traditions describe the Archons as testing souls before allowing them to ascend.

If breaking the curse represents Judas's triumph, then this could be understood as his own resurrection—not in a bodily sense, but in a spiritual transfiguration. Theosophy often describes higher beings as those who have transcended ordinary human experiences, stepping into their true divine nature. Judas may have had to endure the death of his false identity (the betrayer) and the resurrection of his true self (the 13th ruler of the Aeon).

In Theosophical and esoteric traditions, being cursed, tested, or condemned is often an initiation into higher wisdom. If Judas was truly the 13th Daimon, his condemnation could have been a deliberate initiation—a trial he needed to endure before ascending to his destined role. His breaking free would not be mere redemption, but a spiritual victory over falsehood, akin to the resurrection of higher consciousness.

The Martyrdom of Judas

In my journeys, it was revealed to me that Judas did not kill himself but was stoned to death. In the *Gospel of Judas*, Judas knew he would be persecuted and killed. Judas shares with Jesus a disturbing vision he had: *"In the vision I saw myself as the twelve disciples were stoning me and [45] persecuting [me severely]."*

By Judas knowing his fate of being persecuted and killed, he went to his death for his belief in Jesus. This makes Judas not only a martyr but the very first martyr within the context of Christianity. A remorseful death by suicide and a heroic death as a martyr are entirely different narratives.

Martyrs are those who sacrifice their lives serving humanity in the name of God; those who willingly suffer death rather than renounce their beliefs; those who endure great suffering on behalf of a cause, such as salvation. If Judas truly is a martyr, what was he willing to die for? Did Judas navigate his martyrdom, not as an everyday man, but as an initiate of Jesus? Is Judas willing to sacrifice his life more evidence of the immense and powerful being he is to rule over the 13th Aeon?

The *Gospel of Judas* brings to light some intriguing contemplations about martyrdom and sacrifice. Mainly, the gospel brings to question whether the very essence of martyrdom and sacrifice are in alignment with the True God or the false gods. According to the *Gospel of Judas*, the followers of Jesus misunderstood sacrifice, martyrdom, and suffering and believed that their own suffering and martyrdom would bring them their salvation. Their understanding of sacrifice, martyrdom, and suffering led to behaviors that not only served the false gods but betrayed the True God. In essence, the author of the *Gospel of Judas* believes that all martyrs die at the hands of the false gods as the True God does not ask for blood. Just because someone is a martyr does not mean they will become 'perfect' as sacrifice and martyrdom will not save the human soul. In fact, denouncing such deeds of pure madness, standing against the violence and error in thinking is essential in salvation (Pagels et al., 2008, p. 56).

There are two passages in the *Gospel of Judas* that are interesting to contemplate together. In one passage discussed above, Jesus asked the disciples to stand if they were 'perfect,' and they could not stand. In another passage, Jesus told his disciples to *"Stop sac[rificing]"* (Judas 41). Yet, the disciples are so adamant about sacrifice that they talked back to Jesus; they stood in defiance of Jesus's teaching because non-sacrificial views were blasphemy to them. It is fascinating to compare the two passages. The disciples could not face Jesus when he called for the 'perfect' human, but they had the strength, conviction, and willpower to stand against Jesus and defend their practice of sacrificing. They could not stand with Jesus in his glory, perfection, and alignment to the True God but could stand against him as they were aligned to the practices of the false gods.

Was the author of the *Gospel of Judas* attempting to communicate that what disabled the disciples to stand when Jesus asked for the 'perfect' human, as well as what enabled them to stand for sacrifice were both based on the influence of the false gods? Was the author of the *Gospel of Judas* communicating that it is possible to be caught in a matrix of the lesser gods; to exist in the field of consciousness that falsely leads us to believe that sacrifice leads to salvation, while all along it only serves the lesser gods; that being under the influence of the lesser gods can lead us to be in allegiance, in an alliance, in obedience to them and therefore manipulated into thoughts and behavior that serve them while at the same time blind us to the truth?

What are the consequences of critical misunderstandings about the very nature of sacrifice and martyrdom, how we connect with God, and how we comprehend our very lives and afterlife? These can be central components of our human experience, and having these understandings incorrect can be grandly significant to one's entire existence. If one believes that their suffering would lead them to salvation, could their suffering instead lead them further into confinement? If martyrdom does not glorify the True God, what happens when one offers their life as a martyr? If one dies for the false gods, is their soul fodder for the matrix that strengthens the false gods? If we are tapped into the matrix of the false gods, can we be convinced that dying for our beliefs brings salvation when all along it does not? Martyrs thought that they could earn eternal life, but what did they ultimately achieve?

This reminds me of the journey I had of the True God and the false gods where certain souls stayed within the context of the Earth. For some souls, it was a closed system where they were in endless cycles of death and rebirth from the fabricated heaven to the fabricated Earth, and then back to the fabricated heaven only to repeat the cycle. Other souls were able to exit the closed system of the fabrication and reach the True God after their souls departed their physical bodies at the time of death. Could Judas's life, death, and martyrdom be opening the trap doors on the closed system to allow souls to exit and find the path to the True God?

If martyrs sacrifice their lives in service to humanity, could Judas's sacrifice and martyrdom have been for the salvation of humankind? Did he offer his life to free us from the illusion of martyrdom as a path to the True God? Have we, in misunderstanding sacrifice, betrayed our own divinity—while Judas, all along, was only betraying falsehoods? Could his sacrifice have been a key to unraveling the entanglements of deception, opening the way to truth? And was such an act—the ultimate defiance of illusion and the ultimate alignment with truth—the work of the 13th God?

Sacrifice and Sacredness

Sacrifice is commonly seen as offering something (food, objects, life) to Divine beings as an act of propitiation. The offering is to gain the favor of the Divine being or God by doing something that pleases them. Yet, does a True God need to be pleased? Can we ever fall out of favor of a True God?

I have come to understood sacrifice very differently. To me, a sacrifice is an act of making something sacred, be it our lives, our relationships, our connection to Spirit. Sacrifice is about sanctifying our lives; making all aspects of our lives sacred. If I am to sacrifice a meal, I am doing so to make the act of eating more sacred and conscious. Through such actions, I can feel my connection to Creator growing. When I wane in any practice of making my journey scared, I do not feel that I have displeased God or fallen out of favor. I do, however, feel that my connection to God is not as strong.

Within my contemplation about Judas, I have wondered about the specifics of sacrifice. When is a sacrifice in alignment with sacredness, and when is a sacrifice out of alignment? Can we unconsciously sacrifice ourselves to false gods through our thoughts, beliefs, and actions? If so, what knowledge do we need to have that makes any sacrifice sacred and not in vain? Can Judas, as the 13th God, help us to understand when and how sacrifice is sacred? Can he help us know when a sacrifice brings about real and divine sacredness versus fodder for a matrix or anything false?

It is one thing to die; it is another to be cursed, dammed, and shattered. I think about Judas sacrificing his life, and the curse he endured. By Judas offering his body and soul, what did Judas 'make sacred' in his sacrifice? If Judas made an ultimate sacrifice, do we understand the scope and enormity of his actions?

Reorganization of the Cosmos

I do feel that the most powerful souls have not only endured the most challenging places; they emerge out of the darkest voids transformed and able to be great leaders and healers. As Jesus taught Judas about the structure of the heavenly realm, how this world came into being, and how the lower gods rule over it, did Jesus also explain to Judas his purpose during his martyrdom as well as provide guidance on becoming the 13th God?

In the *Gospel of Judas*, some passages lend themselves to portraying Judas as a ruler:

> Jesus said, *"You thirteenth spirit, why do you try so hard? But speak up, and I shall bear with you"* (Judas 44).
>
> *Already your horn has been raised, your wrath has been kindled, your star has shown brightly, and your heart has [...]. [57]*

> *"You will become the thirteenth, and you will be cursed by the other generations—and you will come to rule over them. In the last days they will curse your ascent [47] to the holy [generation]."*

These passages led me to envision Judas speaking as a prophet would speak while being held up and supported by Jesus. I imagine his raised horn as a ram's horn, the kind used as a trumpet. In the *Gospel of Judas*, Jesus tells Judas that he is to lead the "great generation of Adam" back to the position they held prior to the influence of the false gods (Judas 57). The generation of Adam are the people, like Jesus, who have the divine spark present in their being. They come from the True God and the divine realm. As their leader, Judas guides them back to the True God, to where they were before the reign of the inferior gods. Judas's soul is the guiding star leading the way in the exaltation of the great generation of Adam, assisting them in reclaiming their sacredness.

In the *Gospel of Judas*, the author details a gnostic vision of the reorganization of the cosmos. Judas helps to set in motion a series of events that will lead to this grand restructuring.

> *"The current rulers, led by Ialdabaoth and Saklas, will be overthrown; even the stars that are associated with them will be destroyed. Judas will take their place as ruler of the material cosmos, while the saved people will enter the spiritual kingdom"* (Brakke, 2015, p. 36).

After this restructuring, Judas will rule as the 13th daimon, in the highest level of heaven. In my visions, I saw Judas entering a high level of heaven, far past any realm I could enter. I can easily imagine Judas as the 13th God and envision Judas: guiding us into our hearts and an expanded state of being; helping us enter a new consciousness by supporting the integration of our wounds and alchemizing our light and dark into oneness; helping us get honest with ourselves, that we cannot access wholeness while leaving aspects of us in the dark; helping us break out the illusion that we don't even need to do the inner work at all and the delusion of spiritual bypassing being a pathway to enlightenment; showing us how to be the portals to Eden and anchor heaven on Earth; helping us endure the labor of birthing and initiating our remembrance of our True Divinity; and ultimately bringing forth the New Human that can live on the New Earth.

The Infinity of Judas

The image of the infinity symbol came a few times in my visions and has become a way for me to ponder Judas's complexity. In the journeys, I felt the center point of the infinity symbol anchored in my heart and the two loops extending out to my left and right sides. In my journeys, I could feel the energy moving through the symbol, swirling from one side to the other, encompassing all that is. If I ever needed support, Judas helped me anchor in my heart, in the middle, as he represents and embodies the medicine of the middle.

It is fascinating to contemplate how the portrayal and stories of Judas cover the full spectrum of dark and light. Judas has been seen as a tragic hero and a devoted disciple; a villain and a protagonist; a cursed man and a prophet; a tool of the lower gods and a High Initiate of the True God. His name has been used to promote anti-Semitism, and he has been seen as the most trustworthy disciple of Jesus, a Jewish man.

Even the way the *Gospel of Judas* is interpreted stretches the continuum. Some interpret the gospel as saying Judas is of the mortal race; others say he is part of the immortal race. Some say he is from the True God; others say the false god. Some say he is the 13th demon and others claim the 13th god. Some say he will surpass all others and rule over them as a god, while others say he surpasses them in being evil. Some say the *Gospel of Judas* is a parody, while others say it is a prophecy (Judas will lead to the dissolution of the existing world; Judas will become the ruler of the 13th Aeon, the highest level of heaven).

Is Judas good, or is he bad? Does he have access to heaven, or is he stuck in the lowest levels of hell? Why all the extremes? Judas brings great debate. As with most sacred intensities, a higher degree of consciousness may be birthed through the process of anchoring into our knowing as we sort through the controversies.

Perhaps seeing him as an ambiguous figure is very suitable as maybe Judas encompasses all of what is, which is why we cannot figure him out. The interpretations of Judas swirl around and around through the infinity symbol. If I pause in the center, for a moment of knowing without attachment, what is the teaching? In my journeys, as the energy swirled through the infinity symbol, it was moving through all possibilities. Judas Christ was in the middle, he was both the light and the dark, and in being both, he was also beyond.

It is fascinating that the word daimon is neutral within the context of gnostic texts. Daimon has been used to indicate both angels and demons who lived and operated within our universe. Daimons are ruling spirits who are superior to mortals. The higher gods would delegate the work of running lower worlds to daimons (Brakke, 2015, p. 35-36). In the *Gospel of Judas*, the word daimon is used only once, so people interpreting the gospel don't have more than one reference to this word. Hence, they can more easily attribute a positive or negative connotation to daimon. Since in my visions, I saw Judas well beyond me in high levels of heaven I could not access, I attribute the positive version of daimon to Judas.

There are disparities within the ancient texts related to the coins Judas supposedly received. Some say copper, and some say silver. Some believe that the author of the *Gospel of Matthew* used the passages from Zechariah 11:12-13 to concoct the story of the 30 pieces of silver (Mathew 26:14-15, Pagels et al., 2008, p. 18). The dichotomies of the gospels make us wonder if Judas returned the money to the priests (Matthew) or bought a field with the money (Acts). Was Judas killed on this field, or did he take his own life? If Judas knew he would soon be killed, why take any money? What are those coins truly about; have we been bought, has our consciousness been bought?

Some believe Judas was the brother of Jesus. Could they also have been two halves of the same soul or mirror souls? I am sure my Catholic grade schoolteachers would roll over in their graves if they knew I even dared to ask such a question. Perhaps this is exactly what we need to do; roll over in our graves; awaken from our slumber; push the limits of consciousness by asking such questions. Regardless of the answer, we can break the barriers of thought by asking. Let's consciously go off the deep end and push the notion of sacrilege off the ledge.

Within gnostic writing, there are teachings about the splitting our human perfection of unity into that of duality represented as Adam and Eve. By Judas carrying the medicine of the middle, can he anchor in a path as we find our way back to Eden, back to wholeness? It is one thing to hold the concept that we have a divine aspect of ourselves. It is another thing to marry this part of ourselves as a lived experience. To me, Judas embodies the reunion of Adam and Eve, our humanity with our divinity. He represents the return to Eden—not as a place we lost, but as a state of being we are invited to remember while still in form.

Symbolically, I see Judas on one side of the infinity symbol and Jesus on the other, much like the left wing and the right wing belonging to the same bird. However, I do not feel Judas as the opposite of Jesus, as if one symbolizes light and the other dark. Instead, they feel like partners in the consciousness of liberation where Jesus supports us to remember we are divine, and Judas helps us marry that divine part of ourselves; Jesus helps us awaken to our divinity; Judas helps us integrate it. Together, they guide us home—not to an external paradise, but to the sacred wholeness within ourselves.

Judas and the Unfinished Tikkun

In Kabbalah, the concept of *tikkun* (repair) is central, representing the ongoing process of restoring harmony and balance to the cosmos. It is believed that human actions, both individual and collective, contribute to this repair by transforming spiritual fragmentation into wholeness. Some mystical interpretations suggest that Judas carried a unique role in this cosmic process of healing and transformation. Rather than being a betrayer, he may have been an instrument of divine will, participating in a larger, hidden purpose beyond human judgment.

If Judas's name and actions were misunderstood—if the true nature of his role was distorted through history—this could create an unresolved energetic charge in the collective consciousness—one that might still seek resolution today. In Kabbalistic thought, unresolved energies, especially those tied to injustice or misinterpretation, can linger across generations, seeking rectification. A distortion in the collective consciousness may have manifested as:

The Deep-Seated Fear of Betrayal – Judas as the archetypal traitor may have reinforced a deeply ingrained fear of being deceived by those closest to us. This fear, embedded in relationships, institutions, and even spiritual traditions, fosters separation and suspicion rather than unity.

Scapegoating and Collective Guilt – Within the collective consciousness, Judas represents the need to assign blame for suffering. Humanity has spent millennia using him as a scapegoat, mirroring a broader pattern in which societies label and exile individuals as the cause of their problems. This process may fuel cycles of injustice, as history repeats itself through new scapegoats—minorities, dissidents, or perceived enemies.

The Weight of Collective Condemnation – If an entire generation—or multiple generations—believe someone is cursed, their collective projection may act as an energetic barrier, keeping the soul or its imprint in a state of exile. Theosophy and Kabbalah suggest that what we hold in consciousness affects not only individuals but the greater spiritual ecosystem. If humanity has condemned Judas for over 2,000 years, is there a lingering spiritual fracture in need of repair within the collective?

The Corruption of Truth – Judas's story can be imprinted into the collective consciousness as a representative of how entire belief systems can be built on distortion. This has major implications—not just for Christianity, but for how collective narratives shape reality. It raises the question: How many other stories, taken as absolute truth, are actually built on deception or manipulation?

The Suppression of Hidden Knowledge – If Judas was part of a deeper divine plan, then his vilification may symbolize a broader pattern of truth being concealed or distorted to serve external narratives. Restoring his true role could be part of the greater tikkun—not just for his name, but for the recovery of spiritual wisdom that has been lost or suppressed.

The Question of Redemption and Liberation – Judas' condemnation has set a precedent that some betrayals are unforgivable. His story cements the idea that some figures must bear eternal blame, preventing true healing and reconciliation. Perhaps humanity, too, must break free from the weight of its own projected judgments to step into a new paradigm of redemption and liberation.

The Power of Archetypes to Shape Reality – Archetypes, once embedded in the collective consciousness, may influence human behavior on a massive scale. The belief in Judas as the betrayer has reinforced dualistic thinking—good vs. evil, loyalty vs. treachery—when reality is often far more complex.

It is possible that humanity has spent two millennia reinforcing a false narrative that has shaped fear, blame, and separation in profound ways. Imagine what would shift if this story were rewritten—if the archetype of betrayal were re-examined, and the collective consciousness freed from a false weight.

I believe that this unfinished tikkun calls for healing—not just for Judas, but for humanity. Revisiting his story with an open heart and a new perspective—one that recognizes his possible role in tikkun—may help dissolve lingering energetic imbalances in the collective consciousness. This could lead to a deeper reconciliation of an unresolved imprint that continues to shape humanity's spiritual evolution, influencing religious narratives, moral frameworks, and personal struggles with trust, loyalty, and betrayal.

Judas's very name signifies a gateway to the sacred mysteries of the Divine. The name Judas is the Greek translation of the Hebrew name Judah. In Hebrew, Judah (יהודה) contains the divine name יהוה (YHWH) with the addition of the letter ד (Daleth)—a letter that symbolizes a doorway. Daleth is also the first letter of Daath, the hidden sphere in the Kabbalistic Tree of Life, representing secret knowledge and divine wisdom.

Far from being merely a symbol of betrayal, Judas may be the key to unlocking lost wisdom—an initiator guiding us beyond illusion and into higher realization. If we free Judas from the false weight imposed upon him, we may also free ourselves from the distortions that have shaped human consciousness for millennia. Perhaps the ultimate tikkun is not only the restoration of his name but the restoration of truth itself—leading humanity toward a deeper relationship with trust, destiny, and the divine.

Holy Hell

> *There is no coming to consciousness without pain. People will do anything, no matter how absurd, in order to avoid facing their own Soul. One does not become enlightened by imagining figures of light but making the darkness conscious.* ~ Carl Jung

To me, the second coming is not an event but a period of time of us coming into wholeness, a time where human consciousness shifts dramatically and expands the way we perceive ourselves and the nature of reality; a time of truth and transparency. Some believe that before the second coming, there will be a time of intense darkness. If intense darkness is truly coming before the light, perhaps it is the darkness of the collective mind (where we have fed into it fear, violence, distortion, and forgetfulness); the darkness of our shadows returning to us individually; the darkness of the womb that will give birth to the New Earth. Maybe what we perceive as increased darkness is an uncovering of that which already exists and is in need of integration.

If there is indeed an increased level of darkness, perhaps this is not to be feared, avoided, or confronted but embraced. Perhaps there needs to be a shift inward and a subsequent reorientation to the relationship with darkness; a change from being fearful to understanding, from believing darkness needs to be avoided and that if we go there, we will be trapped forever—to knowing that it is the darkness that sets us free. Our pathway to paradise, to anchoring heaven on Earth may be developing a new relationship with darkness based on alchemy; learning how to turn our fear into power, our anger into change

I feel that as we become skilled alchemists, we comprehend how to work with the darkness. This powerful force may no longer seize us if we learn how to wield our swords of true alchemists swimming in the creative energies of the dark womb. If we know how to work with these energies, perhaps we will no longer be overcome but in awe of the creative forces that can be birthed.

Just as white light contains all wavelengths of the visible spectrum, true transcendence requires the integration of all aspects of existence—light and shadow alike. White is a mixture of all colors in roughly equal proportions. To go to the light, we have to take all of the colors with us, not just the colors we like. It is through this embrace of wholeness, of the full range of our human experience, that we find the path forward. Transformation does not come from bypassing the darkness but from standing at the center of all that is, alchemizing fear into wisdom, and allowing the creative forces of the unseen to guide us toward the birth of something new.

To me, Judas offers a deepening of our relationship with darkness and, therefore, wholeness. I believe he is available to help us do the deep down, wretchedly hard shadow work, the work that brings a depth of salvation we have yet to experience as he is master of triumphing over any matrix, a master of breaking free, a master of transforming darkness. I believe that bringing the darkness into wholeness is the highest work we can do. That there is a holiness in doing our shadow work; a liberation from healing trauma, from processing grief, from entering the dark places of our hearts. It is from going to hell and back, from diving deep into our misery and transforming it, from facing the very parts of us that we are most afraid of that we can be the freest.

Darkness is a place where we can hide pieces of ourselves that are frightened, as well as parts we are too scared to face. There is sophistication and intelligence in leaving aspects of ourselves in the dark, not only for its protection but also for ours. We can face things when we are ready to meet them. We can bring them to light when it is safe for us to do so. Sometimes it is too much for us to feel, or it is not even safe for us to because we have to deal with the intensity of a given moment or span of time.

To bury an aspect of us is not always denial; it can be survival. Yet, we can forget that we buried something. We get used to living without this part of ourselves. Then we may see these aspects of ourselves as foreign, as part of the underworld, as something we need protection from. As these lost parts of ourselves long to come back to us, they can be lost and frightened, and we can be frightened of them. The pieces we have placed in the dark seek us; they seek the part of us that remained in the light. As we welcome these pieces, I believe we heal our hearts and become more and more whole.

We can actively avoid the dark, yet we seek it; if we seek wholeness, we seek what we left in the dark. It is quite the paradox: we can avoid the darkness, yet we seek wholeness, and without incorporating our shadows, we cannot obtain wholeness.

Have some of us been misled into thinking that we are to exit the matrix when all along our freedom is in entering the darkness of its constructs and working our magic as alchemists? Do we Exit or Enter? Is the exit in us? To exit, do we need to exist fully? When we enter fully into existence, is that our freedom? The letter 's' looks similar to an infinity symbol. It is fun to see that when we add an 's' (infinity) to the word exit, the word exist arrives. Is our true empowerment and enlightenment attained not by walking towards the light but by entering the light via the black baptismal fire where we welcome all, accept all, and embrace all?

I wonder if evolutionary wise, we are metaphorically at the intersection of the 'stairway to heaven' and 'the highway to hell,' I wonder if it is time not to take either road but rest at the intersection and embrace all roads. At this intersection, is Judas there waiting for us? Has he broken ground, set up camp, lit a fire, and is waiting for us, with his medicine of the middle? Perhaps we stop trying to tread upon the path of enlightenment, thinking it is up the stairs to heaven rather than at the intersection. Perhaps Judas is inviting us to rest at this intersection and embrace all there is, to end our exhausting quest for truth by being in our knowing that we are connected to all of existence.

The Star of Judas

In the *Gospel of Judas*, Jesus tells Judas that his star will lead the great generation of Adam away from the inferior gods and towards the eternal realms of the True God. Judas's soul is the guiding star. In an afternoon daydream, I envisioned the Fruit of Life as a representation of Judas's star. The Fruit of Life has been described as the blueprint of the universe, supporting the fundamentals for all life from the construct of atoms to the molecular composition of everything in existence. The Fruit of Life is made of 13 circles, which is one reason why I thought it could represent Judas's star. Judas was no longer within the ranking of the 12 disciples who were under the dominion of the 12 lower rulers. Instead Judas became the 13th disciple on Earth, who was destined to rule over the 13th Aeon in the heavens.

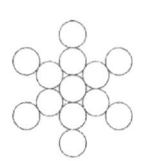

The star is made of a trinity of lines, with each line being made with five circles. This reminds me of my vision of tree blossoms of five petals growing in clusters of three to five flowers. To me, the three lines of the star represent the trinity of matter, spirit, and soul: matter (Earth), spirit (Heaven), and soul (collective human soul). I envision the central line running north to south as the line representing the human soul, while the other two lines represent matter (Earth) and spirit (Heaven). Each line carries the Pentad of Divinity (represented in the five circles of each line), including the Father, the Son, the Holy Spirit, the Divine Mother, and Judas.

I imagine the five circles of the central line representing the human soul and our evolution. When our soul is fully activated, when we align with our divine spark, we metaphorically embrace all five circles of our line. I feel we are evolving to embody our true divinity and ponder what happens when we reach a place where we can embrace our total capacity. In this central line with all five circles activated, do we function as we are divinely designed to and enter the truth of our star-like nature and become portals to Eden?

What is the work of the soul within the context of our galaxy? We speak about connecting heaven and Earth, but what is connecting them? Are we the fulcrum with which these realms connect? Does Heaven connect to Earth through our souls? In Judas's star, the three intersecting lines link the heavenly realm to the material realm through us. Similar to the infinity symbol, where all of existence is united, this star metaphorically links together different levels of consciousness, matter and spirit, through us.

When I think about our role within the context of existence, I do not believe we are special, nor do I think we are insignificant. This is not to make us ultra important in our human roles, but to ponder, are we stepping into our divine roles and understanding our purpose within the larger context of creation, of all that is? We are connected to all that is. Just as our emotional, mental, physical, spiritual levels are connected and cannot be separated, we are connected to the environment in which we live. Our environment is connected to the Earth, which is connected to the solar system, which is connected to the galaxy, which is connected to the universe. Not one level can be separated from another level, regardless of how large or small. Is the collective of our human souls significant within the context of all that is? I am not asking because I think we are essential or necessary; I am asking because if we have a role, how do we best show up for our galactic jobs, and is this something the essence of Judas can assist us with?

Ultimately, I wonder how our human evolution is connected to the Earth, the heavens, and beyond. What is the global and even universal impact of the advancement of the human soul? Within the notion of as above so below, is there a middle: is heaven above, the Earth below, and our collective human soul in the middle? When we are able to stand on the middle ground, allow for all existence to run through us, be accepting of all that is, be in total union and wholeness without exclusion, are we then able to enter the Eden of remembrance, wholeness, and unity that we once parted? What happens to the universal flow of energy when we are in correct alignment to all that is; remembering our divinity, our true nature, our connection to the True God?

Can Judas's star, his very soul, be one of the many guides available to help us understand ourselves not just as human beings but as universal beings?

Friday the 13th, Holy Days of Remembrance

The calendar year is broken into 52 weeks and the four seasons of winter, spring, summer, and fall. Each season is 13 weeks long. Though there is a seasonal rhythm to the number 13, Friday the 13th does not have such a rhythm. Though Friday the 13th happens more often than any other day and date combination throughout the calendar year, it does not occur in a rhythm like yearly holidays such as New Years'. To me, there is something magical about this lack of rhythm. I feel I can be in routines / ruts that do not serve me and sometimes breaking the pattern entails breaking a rhythm. What if these seemingly random days can keep us on our toes, a bit more alert, than some of the rhythms / habits that can drum us to sleep?

Has the number 13 and Friday the 13th been interwoven into the magic of creation all along? According to numerology philosophy, 13 represents a sense of renewal, passion, motivation, and significant accomplishments. In the name of Judas Christ, is it time to make Friday the 13th the Holy Days of Remembrance, Holy Days that occur in a non-rhythmic way in our calendar year that helps us break out of nonbeneficial rhythms?

Discerning Light from Illusion

It has been fascinating to write this book about Judas while the experiences and events of 2020 unfolded as they did. It has been fascinating to witness how people relate to truth, not only as it pertains to the news but also to the path of ascension. It makes me wonder how the essence of Judas can help us navigate our everyday lives during such a complex time; a time where it is extra challenging to discern what is real, factual, and truthful as it relates to fundamental aspects of our lives. We face many conflicts over truth within our political, educational, and medical realms, to name a few. A crucial area to navigate with truth is the evolution of our very souls and the planet.

During these times, I feel it is essential to recognize how easily darkness can disguise itself, even in the pursuit of truth and awakening. If we are not mindful, the very pursuit of light can unknowingly perpetuate the very patterns we seek to transcend. True evolution requires deep discernment—not only of external narratives but also of our own beliefs, biases, and emotional responses.

It is crucial to recognize that we can sincerely believe we have found the truth while still being misled. True discernment requires us to be both keenly aware and deeply reflective, mastering our own evolution rather than assuming we have arrived at absolute understanding. Without this level of awareness, what we expect to be a reality of peace and freedom could instead become an illusion that keeps us bound in deception.

As we collectively dream of a glorious future, I feel it is imperative that we take full responsibility for where we are as well as where we are heading. This responsibility requires an ability to discern frequency; to decipher the vibrations with which we are creating. Without this discernment, we risk being deceived by the darkness as it presents itself as the light. However, by staying connected to the wisdom of our hearts, we can navigate beyond deception and into true clarity. Perhaps Judas offers a reminder of this—urging us to sharpen our perception so that we do not lose our way.

We are wired as human beings to be socialized into the norms and the myths of our culture; it is part of our survival. Therefore, our notion of reality can not only feel like our truth but what is true in general. I feel it is the work of the soul to reach beyond the ideas and notions that have been presented to us, as it can be easier for us to be socialized into a culture than to break free of our indoctrination.

I honor the difficulty in the pursuit of truth as the stories we grew up with can feel so factual that there is no need to question them. If falsities have persuaded us, then when the truth is presented, it can feel like a nonsensical myth that is easy to deny. Understandably, we may reject any evidence of truth because when falsities are presented to us, they are presented to us within the context of the information being true. When we live in separation from our inner authority, an illusion can be our master, our authority. If someone comes along to show us our illusion, they can be seen as a heretic or insane. I feel that it is not that our ego cannot handle what we believed in is not valid; it is possible that we don't even know to question because the falsity often feels so real. Misconceptions can dampen our pursuit of truth or even prevent us from being on a path to pursue truth because we may have been captivated by the stories we have been told.

Judas as a Guide in the Pursuit of Truth

When thinking about Judas and how he may be assisting humanity, I reflected upon the words of *Plato, "Those who are able to see beyond the shadows and lies of their culture will never be understood, let alone believed, by the masses."* I feel Judas sees beyond the shadows and lies. He is not understood, let alone someone viewed as a being we can believe. Yet, he might be a guide helping us connect to our inner knowing so that we can navigate forward on the path of truth.

I don't claim the ultimate truth about Judas, but I do proclaim my truth about him. I believe Judas is helping us to connect our humanity and divinity, our Adam and Eve, and ultimately heaven and Earth. I believe Judas made the ultimate sacrifice and performs a vital role in human ascension. Judas provides the medicine of the middle, the middle road that alchemizes both light and dark within us as we move toward true wisdom.

Judas serves as a profound mirror, reflecting humanity's deepest shadows and unconscious betrayals. Rather than being a traitor, he embodies the archetype of one who catalyzes transformation by revealing what we most resist facing. Judas forces us to confront our own capacity for self-betrayal and projection and reclaim our inner authority.

His presence in the story of Jesus invites us to examine the illusions we uphold, the ways we reject truth, and how we externalize blame rather than acknowledge our own inner fragmentation. By holding up this mirror, Judas challenges us to step into radical self-awareness, making him an essential guide in the process of awakening.

If the Crucifixion Never Happened: Beyond Betrayal, Beyond the Cross

Some traditions believe that Jesus was never crucified, while others claim that someone else was crucified in his place. Islamic tradition, based on the Qur'an (Surah 4:157-158), teaches that Jesus was not crucified but was instead raised to heaven, with another person—possibly Judas Iscariot or Simon of Cyrene—made to resemble him and crucified in his place. Some Gnostic sects, such as the Basilidians, also believed that Jesus only appeared to be crucified, with Simon of Cyrene mistakenly executed instead. The Ahmadiyya Muslim movement holds that Jesus was placed on the cross but survived, later traveling to India, where he lived out his life. Certain esoteric and mystical traditions suggest that Jesus' crucifixion was symbolic rather than literal, or that he continued his mission in secrecy after the event.

Additionally, some believe Judas was not a betrayer but a protector—executed for keeping the secret that Jesus was never crucified. If true, Judas sacrificed himself to preserve Jesus's life, making his role not one of treachery, but of profound devotion.

Rereading my journeys through this lens, I realize that nothing fundamentally changes in my interpretations of my experiences. Whether or not Jesus was crucified, the essence of Judas's path remains the same. In my journeys, I have witnessed him fractured, cursed, and condemned to hell, bearing the weight of immense suffering. I have also seen him rise as the 13th God, transcending the torment placed upon him. These experiences still hold their meaning, as they reflect the profound transformation Judas underwent—regardless of the historical details of Jesus's fate.

Through my dreams and journeys, Judas has appeared to me as both a forsaken outcast and an exalted divine being. I have felt the immense sorrow of his isolation, the agony of being misunderstood, and the weight of humanity's condemnation pressing upon him. Yet, I have also seen him break free from that condemnation, emerging as a luminous force—one who has ascended beyond suffering and reclaimed his divine essence.

This suggests that Judas's story is not bound by a single historical moment, but is instead an archetypal journey of betrayal, exile, transformation, and redemption. Whether Jesus was crucified or not, Judas's experience of being cast into darkness, only to later rise in divine sovereignty, remains intact. His path is one of sacred endurance, showing that even the most vilified figures can transcend their imposed fate and reclaim their true power.

If the crucifixion did not happen as traditionally told, it is staggering to consider how much of human history, culture, and belief systems have been built upon a misunderstanding or deliberate alteration of events. Christianity's entire framework of salvation hinges on Judas betraying Jesus, leading to his crucifixion. But if Judas actually saved Jesus and/or died in his place, then Judas would not be the ultimate traitor but the ultimate martyr—someone who bore the weight of eternal disgrace to fulfill a hidden purpose—someone who sacrificed everything, including his reputation, to protect his friend and fulfill a hidden purpose. If he endured torture and death to protect Jesus, accepting unimaginable suffering without seeking redemption or recognition, he would be one of history's most selfless figures as well as the greatest historical scapegoats of all time, all while embodying a supreme act of self-sacrifice.

If Jesus was not crucified, it would only deepen my belief that Judas bore the weight of humanity's rejection to facilitate an extraordinary awakening. He serves as a mirror to our self-betrayals, reflecting the unhealed wounds imprinted on the collective consciousness. His presence is an ongoing invitation to look deeper—beyond dogma, beyond fear, beyond the narratives designed to keep us from confronting our own shadows. In rejecting Judas, humanity has been rejecting its own reckoning, regardless of whether Jesus died on the cross.

No matter the truth of the crucifixion, Judas remains a guide out of falsity and into truth. He can help us dismantle limiting structures that have shaped civilizations in ways that restrict human evolution. He exposes the illusions that have molded belief systems through deception, fear, and power, rather than truth. He highlights our innate tendency to seek narratives that provide meaning—while leading us toward a truth-filled story, one rich with the potential for expansion and transformation.

With Judas as an ally, we could pierce through centuries of distortion, uncover hidden truths, and separate reality from myth. Imagine accessing the unfiltered truth about history, religion, consciousness, and existence itself—beyond manipulation, bias, or personal agendas—by connecting directly to all that is through our hearts.

If we embody a fearless pursuit of truth, willing to challenge everything—history, religion, science, even personal identity—to uncover what *is* rather than what we've been told, I believe Judas meets us there.

If Judas was condemned for an act of ultimate devotion, his name has carried an unresolved energetic wound in the collective consciousness for centuries. Healing this distortion—acknowledging Judas as the protector, not the betrayer—could be one of the greatest acts of spiritual tikkun (repair) in our time.

To me, Judas's purpose and essence are vast and profound. He embodied unwavering loyalty and faithfulness to his divine mission, no matter the cost. Judas understood that he would face severe persecution and be cast into darkness, yet he fulfilled his role with absolute devotion. Knowing that following Jesus's request—whether to protect his life or hand him over—would lead to his own downfall, he remained steadfast in his commitment. This unwavering alignment with divine will exemplifies the true discipline of a disciple.

His courage, determination, conviction, and alignment with his inner knowing reflect a soul willing to endure immense suffering in service to a higher truth. His sacrifice was not an act of betrayal, but of service, surrender, and ultimate faith. He possesses the strength and power not only to withstand the condemnation that followed but also to rise as the 13th God, transcending the weight of his fate to reclaim his divine sovereignty.

Part 4: The Mirror and the Sword

In his work, *The Chameleon Mirror: From Integrating Emotion to Awakening Felt Perception*, Michael Brown refers to Judas as "an authentic facilitator at work." According to Brown, *authentic facilitators* are individuals who assist us with deconstructing our manufactured ego for the purpose of helping us connect with our essence. Authentic facilitators neither want nor need anything from us, yet their presence in our lives can catapult us into deepening our connection with Presence by mirroring the essential inner work required to do so. Authentic facilitators may mirror to us what we are frightened or resistant to facing within ourselves (Brown, page 125).

If we are blessed with an encounter of an authentic facilitator, we may need to prepare ourselves to gaze deeply into the mirror they hold, resisting the urge to flee from the profound opportunity it offers for inner transformation. If we are accustomed to self-deception, authentic facilitators can be unsettling to be around as their presence may catalyze change by invoking a profound self-confrontation, an inner reckoning (Brown, page 125).

Transformation is rarely a solitary endeavor. While we can cultivate deep self-awareness and transformation through healing modalities and other practices, there are moments when the presence of another—a facilitator—becomes invaluable. Authentic facilitators, as Michael Brown describes, challenge illusions, catalyze transformation, and hold up mirrors to our deepest truths. This role is rarely understood in the world.

This chapter explores the nature of facilitation through the lens of Michael Brown's insights, interwoven with my own interpretations of his work, with a specific focus on Jesus and Judas. Though remembered in drastically different ways, both played crucial roles as facilitators—one wielding the sword of truth, the other holding the mirror of our shadow. Their facilitation roles in humanity's spiritual evolution extend beyond time.

The Nature of Authentic Facilitation

To cultivate a sense of wholeness and embody present-moment awareness, we may unconsciously attract individuals who reveal where we are not fully present. When we are blessed with an authentic facilitator in our lives, we might not like them, nor what they are reflecting to us, yet the gift of their presence may be exactly what our souls need to evolve. Sometimes, we need an outer representative to assist us in accessing what we are not seeing within us, namely, unperceived barriers obstructing us from accessing our essence (Brown, page 126).

> An authentic facilitator may share information with us, but is not a teacher. They may council us, but they are not a councilor. They may listen to our interpretations of what we think is happening to us, but they are not a therapist... (Brown, page 127).

Facilitation, in its truest form, is not about guidance in the conventional sense. It is not about advice-giving, teaching, or even healing as we typically understand it. Instead, it is a profound act of mirroring, revealing to us what we are unable to see within ourselves.

> Possibly the most appropriate word to describe the resonance of a facilitator is the word, mirroring. The task of an authentic facilitator is to reflect what we cannot, and in most cases, do not choose to perceive about ourselves. To accomplish this function, they are required to be nothing and nobody. Instead, they become an empty available space, allowing themselves to be filled with the energy of whatever we hide from ourselves. They are as neutral, as clear, and as honest as a mirror. A good metaphor in describing an authentic facilitator is... 'a chameleon mirror'. A chameleon mirror does not use its ability to change its appearance for the purpose of camouflaging itself, instead it uses this ability to reveal to those who come in close contact with it, what they are hiding from themselves (Brown, page 127).

Brown asserts that becoming an authentic facilitator requires becoming "nobody and nothing." This is an extraordinary challenge in a world that conditions us to derive our value from being "somebody or something." To be an authentic facilitator, one must betray this belief system—transcending the ego—to truly serve another. Brown states, "Authentic facilitators are born into this world, not trained by it. They are raised by Life and not by the living" (Brown, page 127). It makes sense that authentic facilitators cannot be trained by a world focused on identity and status.

> Facilitation, in this context, is by its nature ego-destroying, because it is about agreeing to assist others in destroying their manufactured egos. Therefore, only those with an authentic ego death-wish entertain this responsibility (Brown, page 128).

Brown makes a clear distinction between therapists, councilors, healers and authentic facilitators. Though facilitators may have similar attributes such as being kind and providing a space where we feel safe and comfortable, "an authentic facilitator is also required to be rude, insensitive, needy, devious, or seductive; to reflect whatever dysfunctional behavior we are hiding from ourselves." The idea of being facilitated by someone who embodies nothingness and non-identity, can be difficult to grasp, as the world offers little context for understanding what a true facilitator is or does (Brown, page 128).

Being an authentic facilitator in a world that struggles to grasp their role requires unwavering alignment with one's soul and the Divine. This path demands a deep surrender to divine guidance, an unshakable trust in the wisdom of the soul, and the resilience to withstand misunderstanding, rejection, or even resistance. It is not a role for the faint of heart but for those willing to dissolve personal identity in service of a greater truth.

Authentic facilitators, as viewed by Brown, hold no attachment to how they are perceived because they don't have an ego they need to defend. They are neither concerned with being liked nor with maintaining an image of wisdom or virtue. Their task is to embody, however uncomfortably for us, whatever is required for our awakening.

> An authentic facilitator invests no importance in their reputation. When they are carrying out their tasks they are prepared to be hated, despised, misunderstood, harshly judged, and seldom seen,... Who in their right mind wants to voluntarily perform such a task (Brown, page 129)?

This role requires a depth of inner security that transcends external validation. They do not seek to control perception but instead surrender to the role they are given, knowing it is not their personal identity at stake, but the work of transformation itself.

Such a path cannot be learned in theory or mastered through study. As Brown asserts, it is a path of service of divine placement. Those called to it must first undergo a process of deep self-confrontation, dissolving their own attachments and illusions before they are capable of holding space for another. Without this lived experience, they remain unqualified, not by lack of knowledge, but by lack of energetic capacity.

> To enter such a field of play is not something we can study for and be taught to do by another. It is a path of service that we walk upon because it is where our feet are placed by God. To be able to perform this task, we must first learn to be this for ourselves. Until we thoroughly identify, see through, face, and overcome our own possessive plights, we do not contain the physical, mental or felt capacity to facilitate another. We are just not energetically qualified (Brown, page 129).

Judas, to me, was qualified. He was placed by God—just as much as Jesus was—an initiate who had either facilitated his own ego-death or had been guided through it by Jesus himself. His role was not accidental but divinely ordained, requiring an immense depth of inner work. He was not a betrayer, but someone who understood, at the deepest level, the necessity of becoming whatever was required for the greater unfolding of truth.

An authentic facilitator moves energy through themselves without attachment, without mistaking it for their personal identity. This ability is born from direct experience—having faced and transmuted "their own inner demons," they are able to discern what arises from within versus what they are channeling for the sake of another. As Brown describes, facilitation is not about performance or pretending; it is a surrender to whatever role is needed in the moment (Brown, page 129).

> An authentic facilitator is therefore not someone who is just good at the role of pretending; they allow themselves to become whatever role is required to accomplish the task. This aspect of facilitation, this allowing of oneself to become and be possessed by whatever is required to be mirrored in the moment, is an experience impossible for us to allow when our ego is well established. A person with a well-established ego happily takes on a saintly role, but they do not bedevil themselves for the benefit of another (Brown, page 129).

A person with a strong attachment to their own goodness, as Brown suggests, will eagerly play the role of the saint, but few are willing to embrace the role of the damned if that is what is required. Judas, by contrast, accepted the weight of his role—not just in his lifetime but throughout history—knowing he could be reviled for eternity. This kind of surrender is only possible for someone who has transcended their personal ego, who no longer operates from a need to be seen as good or righteous, but instead serves something far beyond themselves.

If we consider facilitation as Brown describes it—where an authentic facilitator does not cling to a fixed identity but allows themselves to become whatever is necessary for the mirror to be illuminated—then Judas was perhaps the ultimate facilitator; someone capable to willingly serve a higher unfolding, even at the cost of his own eternal reputation.

Jesus as a Facilitator: The Sword of Truth

Jesus did not come to bring external peace. His presence, teachings, and actions functioned as a sword, cutting through illusion and compelling people to examine their inner and outer realities. His facilitation was not about comfort but about awakening—challenging the deeply ingrained beliefs and attachments that kept people from truth.

Earlier in this manuscript, I referenced Matthew's gospel in the context of betrayal. It is interesting to see Michael Brown citing the same passage to illustrate Jesus as an authentic facilitator, as well as a similar passage in *The Gospel of Thomas* to describe the "resonance of an authentic facilitator:"

> Do not suppose that I have come to bring peace to the earth. I did not come to bring peace, but a sword. For I have come to turn 'a man against his father, a daughter against her mother, a daughter-in-law against her mother-in-law—a man's enemies will be the members of his own household (Matthew 10:34-36).

Brown asserts:

> This declaration tells us the personality manufactured for Jesus by our traditional Christian religion, that he was a nice person, is inaccurate and misguiding. It is a make believe, saintly mask, that makes it impossible for any congregation member to move through the stages of the unconditionally felt growth that leads to authenticity. Jesus as The Christ was not a nice person; He was a real person as much as He was nothing and nobody. This is why He could charge into a temple, madly cracking a whip, shouting and screaming like a crazed lunatic, overturning tables and chasing out the money-lenders. In that moment He was not angry, but He was anger. Nor was He the slightest bit concerned about His personal reputation; He was mirroring the hidden fear of the money-lenders and the suppressed rage of those whom they abused. He was allowing Himself to be possessed by what they were hiding within themselves. He was being a chameleon mirror.
>
> Jesus was a kind and marvelous God-Realized human being, with a heart big enough to mirror the suffering of the entire planet, but as His above

> words reveal, we would not have wanted to enter His Presence wrapped in a cloak of self-demeaning inauthenticity. If we had, out of His love for us, He would have wielded the sword of truth to mirror what we are hiding from ourselves and to set fire to our illusions, causing a war to break out between our authentic identity and our manufactured ego (Brown, page 130).

Jesus' declaration that He came not to bring peace, but a sword, speaks to the disruptive and piercing nature of truth. Authentic transformation is rarely a gentle process—it demands that we confront the illusions we cling to, and often, this process is painfully uncomfortable.

The nature of authentic facilitation is rarely what people expect. It is not about making others feel comfortable, nor is it about affirming illusions. Authentic facilitators serve by holding a mirror—reflecting not only what is beautiful but also what is painful, unconscious, and unresolved. Their presence disrupts the status quo. Jesus's purpose was not to bring harmony to societal structures but to dismantle illusions, awakening people to a truth they often resisted.

> No one taught Jesus how to accomplish this; He was born into it. His life experience and how He responded to it qualified Him for His destined role. This is why He was disliked by the establishment; not because he was a nice person to be around, but because His level of honesty was not appreciated by those who paid homage to the living but not to Life. Jesus was and still is a chameleon mirror; He

> remains powerful because, in terms of being a personality, He does not exist. He died to being a personality before He began facilitating the world. He appeared as what His disciples and those who came to Him for guidance needed to perceive of themselves to achieve authenticity. He is one of the most profound examples of an authentic facilitator witnessed by humanity in our limited recorded history. Did He leave peace on earth in His wake? No, this was not His intention. No authentic facilitator intends peace on earth; they teach us to be at peace within ourselves as we walk the troubled earth. To this very day, His momentary Presence, timed to deliver humanity into The Piscean Age, continues to wield a sword that brings fire and war to any individual or community attaching itself to an illusion of what they are, and therefore, what God is (Brown, pages 130-131).

Many depict Jesus as a passive figure of peace, but peace was never His goal—truth was. And truth, when it meets resistance, brings division. His words, His presence, and His actions were a sword cutting through falsehood, encouraging people see themselves as they truly were.

This is why Jesus was an authentic facilitator—He did not impose teachings on people, nor did He tell them what they wanted to hear. Instead, He became what they needed to see in order to recognize their own reflection. His existence was not about personal identity, but about embodying the precise energy required to catalyze transformation in others.

Judas as a Facilitator: The Mirror of Betrayal

Judas' presence in the story of Jesus challenges us to look at the nature of awakening: it is not always a process of comfort and grace, but often one of rupture and deep reckoning. Jesus himself declared, *"I did not come to bring peace, but a sword,"* a statement that speaks to the disruptive nature of truth and transformation. In this sense, Judas was an instrument of the same divine force that Jesus served—one who held up the mirror that exposes what is hidden.

Judas's mirror reflects the unexamined shadows within humanity. His actions force us to confront the painful reality of betrayal—not merely in the external sense, but in the ways we betray ourselves, our truths, and our divine nature. The traditional narrative frames Judas as an outsider, an anomaly, yet his story resonates so profoundly because it echoes a universal wound. In vilifying Judas, we externalize our own fears of disloyalty, deception, and abandonment, reflecting humanity's reluctance to acknowledge our own complicity in maintaining illusions, fears, and separation from the divine.

Judas can wield this mirror as effectively Jesus wields a sword because he was not an unfortunate figure caught in the tides of history but an initiated facilitator who understood his role. Judas's actions were not those of a traitor but of a trusted companion carrying out a divinely placed task with full awareness. In accepting his role, Judas bore the weight of humanity's rejection, becoming the scapegoat for our collective resistance to truth. His facilitation, however, was just as essential as Jesus'—without it, the components of awakening could not be complete.

Perhaps the true healing of Judas comes not from forgiving him, but from realizing there was never anything to forgive. He was not the betrayer; he was the mirror. He did not turn against Jesus—he turned humanity toward itself. And in that act, he fulfilled one of the most profound roles in spiritual history. He carried the weight of misunderstanding, exile, and projection not just for himself, but as a function of divine orchestration.

Jesus wielded the sword of truth, cutting through deception and illusion; Judas held the mirror of shadow and self-reckoning, revealing what we do not wish to see. Together they embody the nature of an authentic facilitator (the mirror) and the transformative, often disruptive force they wield (the sword). Together, they serve truth by reflecting what must be seen and by dismantling what is inauthentic. Together, they facilitate a radical awakening that transcends their individual identities.

The Scapegoat and the Shadow

It takes an enormous amount of courage to face what we have concealed within ourselves. As humans, we create intricate defense mechanisms to keep our deepest wounds hidden, often without even realizing it. When we encounter an authentic facilitator—someone who holds up a mirror to what we are not yet ready to see—our first instinct may not be transformation, but resistance. We may glimpse a painful truth and immediately retreat, reinforcing our defenses. In doing so, we often project onto the facilitator, accusing them of having wronged us rather than recognizing the discomfort as a reflection of our own unresolved pain.

Brown describes how, when we are unable to be facilitated, an authentic facilitator may:

> ...voluntarily demean and betray themselves so we feel safe again. The facilitator does this knowing full well we will turn on them, wield blame, accuse them of betrayal, and all manner of heinous atrocities. Of course, all of these dramatic accusations are unfounded and illusionary; they are no different to someone shouting at a movie screen because the film they are watching causes them fear. The main frequency fueling our felt reactions towards the facilitator under these circumstances, is our rage, and a dramatized pretense of being hurt by them in some way. Often, we summon the world to our side to defend our honor so as to distract everyone from what we are running and hiding from; the truth about ourselves. Yet, the only pain inflicted is the shock of us seeing our own frightening shadow (Brown, page 132).

When we are not ready to be facilitated, we may turn on those who reveal what we cannot yet face, accusing them of betrayal, harm, or wrongdoing. But these accusations are not rooted in reality; they are defenses against seeing our own shadow. Judas embodies this dynamic on the grandest scale. His role in the story of Jesus has made him the most infamous "betrayer" in history.

> The facilitator does this knowing full well we will turn on them, wield blame, accuse them of betrayal, and all manner of heinous atrocities.

Judas knew what was coming and yet, was willing to be condemned. He stepped into the role of scapegoat, absorbing the collective inability to face deeper truth. Jesus's crucifixion was meant to reveal the illusion of death—to free us from the fear that binds us to limitation. But this truth was too much to bear. And rather than see their complicity in His death, rather than face the terror of what His sacrifice revealed, people needed someone to blame. Judas became that someone.

> Often, we summon the world to our side to defend our honor so as to distract everyone from what we are running and hiding from; the truth about ourselves.

This is exactly what happened with Judas. For over two thousand years, humanity has rallied against him, condemning him as the ultimate traitor. Humanity was not ready to be facilitated by Jesus's death, so instead of seeing what it revealed, they turned on Judas. They made him the betrayer, the villain, the one who disrupted the story of a comfortable Messiah. His actions forced people to confront a terrifying possibility: that salvation was not an external promise but an internal reckoning. And that was too much.

Judas's story is the story of every facilitator who dares to hold up the mirror of truth. When we are not ready to be guided, we lash out at those who try to guide us. We accuse them of betrayal, of cruelty, of harming us—when in reality, they are only revealing what we cannot yet bear to see. But as Brown reminds us, the pain we project onto facilitators is not inflicted by them.

> Yet, the only pain inflicted is the shock of us seeing our own frightening shadow.

Judas was not Jesus's betrayer. He was humanity's mirror. And for that, we condemned him. Brown goes on to state that, "Whatever we accuse our facilitator of is what we are shown by them about ourselves that we are not yet ready to look at" (Brown, page 132). Brown explains the ultimate realization that comes when we finally transcend our fear:

> When we finally overcome our fear, we perceive the whole scenario in the light of a profound revelation, and we then understand what the facilitator sacrificed to keep us in the game; everything and nothing (Brown, page 133).

This notion of *sacrifice* deeply resonates when reflecting on Judas. He made a sacred sacrifice—not only in his earthly role but in the eternal burden of being misunderstood. His actions catalyzed the fulfillment of Jesus' mission, yet he bore the weight of condemnation for generations. This kind of sacrifice is paradoxical—*everything and nothing*—because while it appears as the ultimate betrayal on the surface, it may, in truth, have been the highest act of service.

Judas as an Authentic Facilitator

Brown challenges us to reconsider the depth of Judas's participation in Jesus's mission:

> A wonderful example of an authentic facilitator at work is of the personality in Christianity we know

> as Judas. Judas was Jesus's closest and most trusted companion. Judas knew Jesus's plan to facilitate His disciples, and the communities in which He operated, into looking into their most terrifying mirror, by His allowing of Himself to be publicly crucified. The public crucifixion was Jesus's demonstration of entering Life by overcoming the fear of death. If we think a human as aware as Jesus was crucified by accident, or that the event was in any way beyond His Will, and that He Himself did not purposely set it up, we completely underestimate Whom and What He is (Brown, page 133).

The notion that Jesus allowed His own crucifixion, rather than being a passive victim of fate, radically reframes the event. His crucifixion was a carefully orchestrated facilitation—an ultimate mirror forcing humanity to confront its deepest fear: death. But Jesus could not have executed this plan alone. He needed someone He could trust completely to play the most reviled role in history.

> Not only did He set Himself up to publicly demonstrate the conscious cleaving of matter from spirit, of dying consciously, but He had Judas as a willing accomplice. This was because Judas was the only one He could trust to obediently carry out the required instructions. Judas, by His actions, also became one of the most profound examples of authentic facilitation, when He embraced the role of, 'the greatest betrayer of all time'. Not until our humanity enters present moment awareness shall we collectively comprehend the magnitude of this act of bravery, love and unfathomable compassion (Brown, page 133).

Judas was not simply an unfortunate participant in history—he was an *initiated* one, fully aware of what he was doing. His act was not betrayal but obedience to a higher will. And yet, his role meant he would be condemned for eternity by the very people Jesus sought to awaken.

Brown's perspective on Judas as an "authentic facilitator" is a powerful reframe that challenges traditional narratives and invites deep introspection. It asks us to consider Judas not as a villain, but as a mirror—a willing participant in a cosmic drama meant to awaken humanity to its own illusions and self-betrayal.

The concept of an "authentic facilitator" suggests one who fully surrenders to their role, even at the cost of their own reputation, comfort, or personal redemption. Judas' willingness to carry out his actions, knowing they would brand him as the greatest traitor in history, reveals a level of surrender few could endure. There is an element of radical selflessness in stepping into the role that invites hatred, misunderstanding, and condemnation.

This path mirrors the journey of Jesus Himself, who also surrendered to a fate that the world could not comprehend. Yet, while Jesus is honored for His sacrifice, Judas is reviled for his. Perhaps this is because Judas' role required him to embody what humanity fears: the experience of being seen as the villain, the force of disruption, the catalyst of transformation. In this light, he is not a betrayer, but an initiator of profound spiritual awakening.

Judas's Kiss: The Mirror of Humanity's Betrayal

Judas's kiss—the moment forever remembered as an act of betrayal—is, according to Brown, one of Jesus's most profound gifts to humanity:

> The power of Judas's kiss on Jesus's cheek is incomprehensible in time. Like us, when we perceive our hidden fears mirrored for us, and therefore run from our initial request to be facilitated, religious organizations also do this by accusing Judas of being a betrayer. No one has betrayed Jesus more since His crucifixion than religious organizations (Brown, page 133).

Many religious institutions, the very entities that claim to uphold Jesus's teachings, have continually distorted His message. Some have upheld power structures that serve ego rather than truth, externalized God rather than revealed divine within, and perpetuated suffering by reinforcing separation rather than unity. The betrayal of Jesus by such institutions is not an event locked in time; it is ongoing.

> Judas is despised by us because his act in that moment, which we called betrayal, shows us, through the intimate beauty of a kiss, what our organized religious groups do to God. Judas mirrors, for us all, the hidden face of our continual betrayal of ourselves, and of God. Judas facilitates us to perceive our lack of authenticity. We therefore hate him. Yet he is nothing and nobody except the revealed personality of our own hidden darkness. Judas's

> kiss is one of Jesus's most loving, most powerful, parting gifts to humanity (Brown, page 133).

Judas did not betray Jesus—humanity betrayed itself. His actions exposed the collective illusion, the ways in which we deny truth, reject authenticity, and project our darkness onto others. And for this, we despise him. He forces us to see our own capacity for betrayal—not just of others, but of ourselves and of the divine within us.

The Price of True Facilitation

> Is it possible to train someone to be as brave as Jesus and to be as shamed as Judas? No person with a healthy ego agrees to be falsely blamed and judged as, 'a disgrace for all of time'. Only one who truly practices unconditional love undertakes such a task (Brown, page 134).

To willingly take on the role of a pariah—condemned and shamed not just in one lifetime, but for eternity—requires a level of love beyond human comprehension. This is why Judas is not just a facilitator; he is the ultimate facilitator. He accepted the weight of false blame to serve something far greater than himself.

Facilitation, in its truest form, is not about making people comfortable. It is not about offering soothing words or reinforcing illusions. It is about exposing the root of suffering, even if it means being hated for it.

> It is easy to train someone how to be nice to others, and how to make them feel comfortable and safe

> in their misery. But then one is missing the point by not bringing light to the true nature of suffering in this world. Real suffering is not the symptomatic conditions affecting us mentally, physically or as felt unintegrated emotions. Real suffering is being unaware that all the discomfort we experience in this world is caused by us (Brown, page 134).

Judas's story continues to facilitate us, even now. His presence in the Christian narrative is not just a historical event but an ongoing mirror, asking us: Where do we betray truth? Where do we reject authenticity? Where do we seek scapegoats instead of facing our own darkness?

Judas's sacrifice was sacred. It was everything, and it was nothing.

> Being an authentic facilitator is a horribly beautiful curse carried in one's heart for the love of God (Brown, page 135).

Rewriting the Myth and Updating the Archetype

The narrative of Judas has persisted for millennia, shaping how humanity perceives betrayal, justice, and redemption. But as consciousness evolves, so too must our understanding of these archetypal figures. If Judas has long served as the scapegoat for humanity's fears, what happens when we embrace him rather than cast him out? When we stop projecting betrayal onto an external figure, we are forced to examine the ways in which we betray ourselves—through fear, self-denial, and resistance to change.

Perhaps the real transformation occurs not when we forgive Judas, but when we recognize that there was nothing to forgive. When we no longer need a betrayer in our mythology, we no longer need to see ourselves as victims of betrayal. In rewriting the myth of Judas, we are also rewriting the way we relate to power, responsibility, and the path of awakening itself. Perhaps the true lesson of Judas is not condemnation, but the recognition that every act of perceived darkness holds within it the potential for illumination.

As consciousness evolves, the archetype of Judas as a betrayer could be more accurately updated to authentic facilitator; an archetypal role of immense sacrifice—one that demands a surrender of personal identity, an embrace of nothingness, and an unflinching willingness to be misunderstood. More specifically, Judas's archetype would be The Mirror of Reckoning—the authentic facilitator who stands unwaveringly in truth, even at the cost of being condemned, one who holds up the mirror so others can see themselves clearly, yet in doing so, becomes the target of their projections, rage, and denial. Unlike the archetype of the savior, who is embraced in the light, the facilitator of reckoning is cast into shadow, bearing the weight of humanity's resistance to transformation.

This archetype demands an immense sacrifice—the surrender of personal identity, the dissolution of ego, and the willingness to be vilified. It is the role of one who disrupts illusions not for personal gain, but for the liberation of others, knowing full well that they will be accused, misunderstood, or even cast out.

To embody this archetype is to accept that facilitation is not about being loved or celebrated; it is about being a catalyst. It is to wield the power of transformation with no expectation of recognition, to embrace the void of nothingness so that others might find themselves.

Jesus, the Timeless Facilitator

Eternal figures like Judas and Jesus continue to facilitate humanity's awakening from beyond the veil. Their roles are not confined to a single moment in history—facilitation transcends time. Just as a teacher may return to guide a student in another lifetime, these facilitators remain present, patiently awaiting the moment when we are ready to receive their lessons.

> To this very day, His momentary Presence, timed to deliver humanity into The Piscean Age, continues to wield a sword that brings fire and war to any individual or community attaching itself to an illusion of what they are, and therefore, what God is (Brown, page 131).

The Piscean Age was one of devotion, sacrifice, and belief in external salvation. It was an era of hierarchical spiritual structures, where faith often required submission to religious authority. Jesus's presence at the dawn of this age catalyzed a shift—He challenged the old ways, exposed falsehoods, and demonstrated that the Kingdom of God was not found in institutions, but within.

The Aquarian Age is one of awakening, self-mastery, and the direct experience of truth. It moves beyond external authority and into inner knowing. This transition, like all transformative processes, is not always smooth or peaceful—it requires us to confront the illusions we still cling to, the shadows we have yet to integrate. Just as Jesus's presence in the Piscean Age disrupted established systems, His ongoing facilitation in the Aquarian Age is guiding humanity toward sovereignty, authenticity, and direct connection to the divine. Just as He once dismantled the idea of a distant, externalized God, His energy now challenges us to release the remnants of dependency and step fully into our own divine nature.

Jesus did not come to bring peace, but to show us how to be at peace within ourselves as we walk through fire. His work is not finished—facilitation does not end with a single moment in history. It continues, reshaping itself to meet the consciousness of the age. As we enter Aquarius, we may come to see that Jesus has been with us all along—not as the figure we constructed in the past, but as the reflection of who we are becoming.

Judas, the Unseen Facilitator

If Jesus facilitated the transition into the Piscean Age, then Judas—His most trusted companion—also played a crucial, albeit misunderstood, role in humanity's spiritual evolution. Through Michael Brown's lens, Judas was not a traitor but an authentic facilitator, one willing to "bedevil himself for eternity" in order to mirror humanity's deepest shadows across ages.

In the Piscean Age, Judas's role exposed the human tendency to project our own betrayals onto another rather than facing our inner fragmentation. His actions forced the disciples—and ultimately the world—to confront the painful truth: that Jesus's crucifixion was not a tragedy inflicted upon Him, but a conscious act of facilitation.

However, humanity was not ready to be facilitated by Judas. Instead of recognizing the mirror he held up, the world "summoned others to its side," as Brown describes, creating a collective narrative that cast Judas as the ultimate betrayer. Through externalization, people could avoid looking at their own capacity for betrayal—not only of others, but of themselves and of God.

Thus, Judas became the scapegoat, embodying what humanity was not yet ready to integrate. His facilitation was rejected, just as many reject facilitators in their own lives when they are unwilling to see the truth about themselves.

But what about the Aquarian Age? If Judas's facilitation in the Piscean Age was met with rejection, his role in the Aquarian Age may be about revealing the deeper truth—one that humanity is finally ready to face.

The Age of Aquarius is about direct knowledge, self-mastery, and the dismantling of externalized authority. It calls for us to integrate the very shadows we projected onto Judas. Now, as humanity moves beyond blind faith and into direct experience, we are more capable of recognizing the lesson Judas offered. He was not the betrayer of Jesus—he was the facilitator of a process that ultimately led to liberation. In the same way, every individual in the Aquarian Age is being called to take responsibility for their own spiritual journey, rather than seeking external saviors or villains.

Judas continues to facilitate by holding the mirror of self-betrayal before us. He asks: *Where do we still project blame onto others instead of facing our own darkness? Where do we reject truth because it feels too uncomfortable?* His facilitation, which was so violently resisted in the past, is now being reevaluated by some. The very act that led to his condemnation is being understood not as an act of betrayal, but as an act of profound, sacrificial love.

Brown's words about authentic facilitators apply to Judas more than almost anyone else in recorded history: *"Not until our humanity enters present moment awareness shall we collectively comprehend the magnitude of this act of bravery, love and unfathomable compassion."*

As we transition into the Aquarian Age—one of self-mastery, direct experience, and inner awakening—humanity may finally be ready to see Judas not as a traitor, but as one of the greatest facilitators the world has ever known. His role in the past was misunderstood, but now, as people begin to embrace self-responsibility and integration, Judas's sacrifice may be seen in its full magnitude.

Come to Jesus: Come to Judas

A *come to Jesus moment* refers to a profound realization, reckoning, or moment of truth—often one of surrender, clarity, or awakening. It is a turning point where we can no longer ignore what has been calling for our attention.

A *come to Judas moment* is a deep reckoning with one's own shadow—the moment when we stop externalizing blame and instead face the uncomfortable truth of our own self-betrayal and the ways we have suppressed or abandoned our own divine nature.

A *come to Judas moment* would not be about seeking comfort but about surrendering to radical honesty. It would mean confronting the illusions we have built around ourselves, the projections we cast onto others, and the ways we resist awakening. This moment would demand that we take responsibility for our own inner crucifixions— the ways we betray, reject, and fearfully sabotage our own Christed essence.

To have a *come to Judas moment* is to stand before the mirror he holds and not turn away. It is to stop running from our own darkness, to cease labeling truth as betrayal, and to embrace the uncomfortable yet liberating process of seeing ourselves as we truly are.

Being Facilitated by Judas

What if we embraced the energy, consciousness, and support of Judas as the ultimate facilitator—guiding us past our denial of our own Christed nature? To accept facilitation at this level is to confront the core illusions we have built around ourselves. It is an initiation into liberation. A baptism in Judas's energy would mean facing the parts of ourselves that resist our divinity.

Judas is not as a force to contend with, or reckon with – but a consciousness that allows us to reckon with ourselves. Judas is not an adversary; he is a mirror. To face him is to face every part of ourselves that denies the truth of who we are.

Being facilitated by Judas would not necessarily be a gentle process, nor one designed to comfort or reassure. Instead, it would be an experience of stripping away falsehood, dismantling self-deception, and revealing the raw truth beneath. To stand before Judas is to face oneself without the safety of illusions. It is to be exposed to the depth of our own resistance, fear, and unacknowledged betrayals. In standing before his unwavering reflection, we are asked: Will we finally see ourselves?

If we were to invite Judas to facilitate our transformation, I imagine his guidance would likely unfold in several layers:

Facing the Shadow Without Projection

Judas holds up a mirror to the aspects of ourselves we avoid—the hidden motives, suppressed fears, and unacknowledged betrayals we have committed against our own soul. When faced with this reflection, our instinct may be to recoil, to reject the mirror and blame the one who holds it. Just as humanity projected its unwillingness onto Judas, so too do we project our discomfort onto those who expose our unhealed wounds. Initially, we may feel anger, blame, or rejection, believing that we are being wronged. But in truth, we are not rejecting Judas—we are rejecting what he shows us about ourselves. His presence reveals where we have abandoned our own knowing, and our resistance is a defense against seeing where we have abandoned our inner truth.

Breaking Through the Illusion of Victimhood

If we seek comfort in the idea that life has wronged us, that we are at the mercy of others, of forces beyond our control—Judas dismantles this illusion with relentless precision. He will expose the places where we have been complicit in our own suffering, where we have handed over our power and then cried betrayal when it was taken. In his facilitation, there is no room for blame.

He would ask, *Where have you betrayed yourself? Where have you abandoned your truth? Where have you abandoned your own knowing?* These questions pierce through our defenses, forcing us to see that we have never been victims—we have always been active participants in our own unfolding.

The Death of the False Self

To be truly facilitated by Judas is to undergo a death—the death of the false self. Judas's facilitation would require the surrender of identity as the small, ego-driven narratives we use to shield ourselves from discomfort cannot survive his gaze. His role is not to comfort us but to demand our absolute willingness to let go. He is not here to reinforce our illusions but to break them apart so that we might awaken to a greater truth. This process is not about external betrayal but about recognizing how we have betrayed our own Christed nature. To move through this initiation is to die before dying—to let go of all that is false so that what is real can emerge.

The Medicine of the Middle

Judas's facilitation is self-reclamation—the awakening to the Christed self that was never lost, only obscured. Just as Jesus's crucifixion revealed the illusion of death, Judas's facilitation reveals the illusion of separation.

Judas stands in the space between—the liminal ground of the medicine of the middle: the alchemical ground where what was once deemed betrayal can be seen as sacred duty, and where condemnation gives way to revelation. The medicine of the middle is the ability to see from an expansive place, where all things can be held in balance. To receive Judas's medicine is to stand in the uncomfortable, raw place where truth exists beyond polarity. In this space, we cease to see ourselves as victims or villains and begin to recognize our participation in the greater unfolding. We stop externalizing blame and instead take full ownership of our role.

To be facilitated by Judas is to be invited into the alchemical process of transformation, where the most painful aspects of our existence are not cast aside but turned into gold. To be facilitated by Judas is to be guided into the fire of transmutation, where we face the uncomfortable truths we often seek to avoid. It is to recognize that our suffering is not punishment but raw material for transformation, and that true liberation is not found in avoidance but in fully embracing our contradictions.

Judas's facilitation is an alchemical one. Just as base metals must endure the heat of the furnace before becoming gold, we too must pass through the fire of self-reckoning.

In the alchemical tradition, transformation requires a dissolution—a breaking down of the old before the new can emerge. Judas's facilitation is a dissolving force. He dissolves illusions, dismantles false structures, and removes the veils that keep us from seeing clearly. Without dissolution, there is no rebirth.

Yet Judas does not leave us in the void. Just as he guides us into the fire, he also leads us through the process of reconstitution. In alchemy, this is the stage where the purified elements come together to form something new. Likewise, after we have surrendered what is false, we are reconstructed in truth. We emerge from the fire no longer bound by the distortions of the past, but as something refined, something greater.

The medicine of the middle is not just about standing between—it is about integration. It is about bringing together the fragments of ourselves that we have cast away. It is to stand in the fire of transformation, to dissolve the illusions that have kept us separate, and to emerge whole. It is to receive the medicine of the middle, the wisdom that sees beyond duality, and to recognize that within us—just as within Judas—there is nothing to be condemned, only something waiting to be reclaimed.

Judas is a timeless facilitator—a steadfast mirror. His name is ever-present in the story of Jesus Christ is no mistake; if humanity did not need his mirror, his name would not be eternally woven into the narrative, ready for us to look into the mirror in any lifetime.

To be facilitated by Judas is to walk through fire, to be stripped bare, to have no illusions left to hide behind. For those willing to step into this initiation, Judas remains, holding the mirror, waiting for the moment when we stop betraying ourselves—and finally see our innate beauty.

When humanity is ready to face his mirror, recognizing the invitation he offers, I imagine the myths and distortions surrounding Judas will dissolve. When we are ready to know our inner Christ, we may no longer need the myth that Judas diminished Jesus into someone who was merely a victim of betrayal. We might unmark Judas as the betrayer of Jesus when we no longer deny the Christ within ourselves. We may no longer need to continue to turn on him, because we turned inwardly. In his restoration, we might just find our own.

Part 5: The CrissCross

My connection to Judas is a complex multidimensional mystery that I pray will be deeply understood one day. In the introduction of this book, I shared how the notion of carrying an aspect / fragment / spark of Judas may explain my experience with him; yet, I continue to ponder the complexity of our interconnection. If a soul agrees to take on a fragment, where is the fragment held; does the fragment reside in the etheric or astral field of the carrier? If the fragment is carried in an energetic field of a person, is there a subsequent crisscrossing or an interweaving of the fragment with the carrier's soul? To what degree can the aspect / spark impact the life of the person carrying the fragment?

I wonder if my connection with Judas impacted my everyday life experiences beyond my dream space. Did carrying a fragment of Judas leave particular imprints in my astral field that then influenced my life in specific ways? In the movie, *Lord of the Rings*, whoever held the ring could be affected by the ring's energy. Similarly, was I influenced by the fragment? Carrying an aspect of Judas that needed healing could explain some of my thoughts, feelings, and life experiences.

In this last section, I share parts of a narrative I wrote in 2017 for the book, *"Pathways of Intentionality. Breaking Open into the Vastness of Devotion."* The manuscript is a compilation of the individual life stories of 13 authors. I wrote my narrative after I had the initial dreams about Judas but before the multidimensional journeys in 2018. My narrative was not a complete autobiography but a condensed version of my life's story, and yet my initial dreams with Judas made it into the pages. Of all the experiences I could have written about in my four and a half decades of life, I shared my dreams with Judas.

When it came time to write this book, I went back to my narrative in *"Pathways of Intentionality"* to retrieve what I wrote about my dreams with Judas. I thought I would only copy and paste the parts related to Judas, which would be all that was worth retrieving for this manuscript. However, when I was scanning the writing, I realized much more of my life story possibly related to Judas. It had been a while since I had written my narrative, so when I reread it with fresh eyes, I was fascinated to see the possible imprint the fragment of Judas might have had on my life. Below are sections of my narrative, along with some reflections.

The title of my chapter, dedication, and opening quote:

"Knowing God as Medicine"

> *I dedicate my narrative to all people who helped me break out of the story in which I held myself. Thank you for having more faith in me than I did in myself. Thank you for seeing the spark I did not see, a kindness I couldn't feel, an intelligence I didn't honor, a potential I couldn't dream of. Thank you for gifting me with a vision of a brighter me than the one I could see - and in doing so, helping me align more fully with my authentic self.*

I titled my narrative "Knowing God as Medicine" as this was the central theme of my story as well as the most significant transformation in my life; a change from feeling separated from God to experiencing God as a profound medicine. The dedication I wrote carried a similarity to Judas breaking out of his story along with being birthed into his authentic self from the help of others.

I started my narrative with these paragraphs:

> **Claiming my story to dissolve my story**
> *There seems to be a continuum from claiming my story to knowing I am not my story. I have experienced denying my story to avoid the pain of transforming it... I have also claimed my story to form my identity. My victim story and my identity were synonymous for many years of my life.*
>
> *Here, on these pages, I wish to share part of my story in the most authentic and vulnerable way that I can with the intent to be helpful to others. I don't want to tell my story in a way that I get bogged down by it or overly identify with it, but in a way that sets me and others free. I want to speak my truth, and at the same time, surrender my story; dissolve my story.*

Rereading these paragraphs through the lens of my experience with Judas was fascinating. From my perspective, there was a denying of Judas's true story on a collective level as well as a knowing that he was not the cultural story created about him. Thus, in my opinion, there was a need to dissolve his false narrative and share his story in the most authentic and vulnerable way that sets him and others free.

After my introduction, I shared part of my life experiences.

> *My grade school class was broken into the cool kids and the not-so-cool kids. I naturally fell into the group of the not-so-cool kids until one day when I was no longer welcomed there. The girls of the not-so-cool wrote me a letter excusing me from their group. After that event, there were the cool kids, the not-so-cool kids, and then me ostracized. I was the outcast of the outcasts. I was made fun of. I was told I was unlovable. I had a speech impediment. I never wanted to speak, and in fact, I could get through the entire day without speaking to anyone. I was there physically, but I had no voice. I lived in isolation, right in the middle of people.*

Judas was ostracized and remains so in many churches throughout the world. He was deemed the outcast of the outcasts and unlovable. To me, Judas was in the stories of the canonical bible but had no authentic voice.

> *I barely wanted to be alive. I was angry at God and jealous of everybody. I had enormous self-loathing and no self-esteem. I was trying my best to show up in life... but as I showed up, so would my misery. We were inseparable - which made life difficult and burdensome.*

> *By the time I was 13 years old, I really couldn't bear living anymore. Life at home was rough. Life in school was hellish, and the only place I felt I had to turn to was death. I thought that suicide would be the best option for escape. In my mind, it felt like a brilliant idea. It was an epiphany - it was my salva-*

> tion from hell. I remember looking at my classmates and thinking this would be the very last time I would see them, and I was delighted at that thought. I went home and took as many medications as I could find in the house and drank as much alcohol as I could, and I thought it would be that easy. I was shocked to wake up and realize I was still alive.
>
> The level of agony was not understandable to me... All I knew at the time was that there was a hell burning inside of me, and the fire was unbearable... It was an internal hell of self-loathing and shame as these circumstances infiltrated every aspect of my being, including my thoughts about myself, the world, and God.

What struck me most in this section was how I described my emotional pain—using the language of agony, an internal hell, and an unbearable fire. I now wonder if these words emerged solely from my own suffering or if they were, in some way, echoes of my connection to Judas and his experience within the consciousness of hell. Could my choice of language have been shaped by an imprint of his pain, woven into my own emotional landscape?

> It is amazing how wounds can infiltrate so deeply and in so many ways: I struggled with commitment because I thought people would abandon me; I would be hyper-vigilant, not fully present in conversations as my mind would be thinking about safety; I was very quiet, and rarely spoke; I had low self-esteem and didn't feel my existence was valid;

I took on the belief that I deserved punishment; my relationship with the Divine was bizarre and distorted at best; I struggled greatly with addictions; disagreements were seen as war and made me very uneasy and afraid; I beat myself up mentally and emotionally as I had learned how to treat myself from how others treated me; I could have the nicest people around me but without the concept of how to receive their love or that I was even worthy of love. So, it was always cold and dark inside of me.

Just being in the world and doing something with my life was difficult... I would bring this heaviness and distortion of reality into life, and things would just go haywire. I had enormous potential but couldn't do anything with it because I also had a programming that I was scum, I have nothing to offer, I am an embarrassment, and should be kept quiet.

In revisiting my narrative, much of it struck me as something that might relate to having an aspect of Judas. If Judas's soul fragmented into many pieces, did the fragment I receive carry aspects of his pain and the curse he endured? I do not feel like a victim of this fragment / aspect of Judas; I simply ponder my connection between Judas and my life experiences. Some people believe that we have past lives and parallel existences. If someone has an unhealed part of them from when they were a slave in another life, this part can impact their current life. Energetically, does it work in a similar way as having a fragment from someone else?

The next section of my narrative is about my relationship with God.

God as Creator and Destroyer

Part of the foundation of my story was my distorted image and understanding of God. I saw him as very masculine, mean, and out-to-get-me. He felt more like the Demon with a destruction story than a God with a creation story. The notion that God is a good God didn't resonate with me. At times, I saw God as evil, dark, distorted, and not worthy of running the universe. When people would say, "Let go and let God" or "Don't worry, God is in control," I would cringe as I did not find relief in such statements. Let God do what to us? Do we really want a wrathful God to be in control?

Hell was tangible to me. When I was in 6th grade, I was digging under a tree in my backyard. Within 6 inches or so, I came across the surface roots of the tree, which were red. I instantly thought that was the entrance to the Devil's home as if hell was that close and that easy to enter. I quickly covered up the roots. This event didn't only shed light on my relationship with God and the Devil, but also on my relationship with nature and creation.

I grew up believing that I have done something so wrong; that my existence is so wrong that there was a good chance that my pack, my tribe, were dwellers of hell, and that this is where I will hang. In both my suicide attempts, I wondered where I would go, feeling hell was definitely a possibility for me.

I attended Catholic school for eight years of my life. It was there I was made fun of and ostracized. I left that school not believing in Jesus or Christianity. I was cold; I was mean; my 13-yearold self basically told beloved Jesus to go to hell. My logic was: if Christians believed in Jesus, and Christians are mean, I don't believe in Jesus. It was there that I was taught that our spirit is a part of God. Yet, I didn't want a God that I didn't like to be a part of me. If my spirit (my essence) is of God, and I don't like God, then I don't like my spirit either. This was the logic of my child self.

If the fragment I carried for Judas had any energy of what he endured, is this how that played out in my life? What was Judas's relationship with God as he journeyed from agreeing to hand over Jesus through the curse he endured afterward?

In my narrative, I wrote about the experience of living under the influence of views from other people. I even title a section, *"Other people holding me in a story."* I believe we held Judas in a story and this untrue narrative had a significant impact on him.

> ***Other people holding me in a story:***
> *I grew up as dum. I had a grade-school teacher that announced in front of the entire class, "You are dumb. D. U. M. Dumb." When a student pointed out that dumb was spelled with a 'b' at the end, she responded by saying, "Kerry is so dumb, she is D. U. M. without the b."*

I attended a small grade school. All the teachers and students knew me. They knew I was slower. They heard me speak with an impediment. They saw me as awkward and unathletic in gym class. My story followed me from one grade to another. And then the story ended. I didn't get smarter overnight. I simply graduated from St. Therese School and started to attend Ossining High School, a large public school. No one knew me there. The teachers were not informed that I was 'dum.' The gym teacher didn't know I was the last one picked when choosing teams. The students didn't know that I was the loser that was ostracized from the less popular group.

My identity wasn't carried in the collective consciousness of the new school. There is a saying, "no matter where you go, there you are." I agree with this very much. For me, it is balanced with external influences. My story is a co-creation of how people see me and how I experience myself in different environments. I often wonder how I am being shaped by environments / people / society and where I am able to maintain myself regardless of the environment / relationship with which I am in.

Over the years, I had a number of friendships fall away as I shifted from one way of being to another. Having others define me was too crippling, and my soul had other destinations than prison within a certain level of consciousness. I have felt trapped in other people's perceptions of me. There have been many friends in my life who have witnessed my instability, my drama, and my intense struggle.

They knew me for this struggle, and it was difficult for me to step into a new way of being when I was around them. I had to end these friendships because I couldn't grow within them...

On the other hand, there have been many people in my life that have had more faith in me than I have had in myself. They saw a kindness I couldn't feel, they saw an intelligence I didn't honor, they saw potential I couldn't dream of. They gifted me with a vision of a brighter me than the one I could see - and in doing so, they helped me step into this potential.

I experienced firsthand the harm of being cast in a fixed narrative, feeling the weight of others' perceptions shaping my identity. This makes me wonder about Judas—how has the false story carried in the collective consciousness for over 2,000 years affected his essence?

In the next section of my narrative, I wrote about feeling stuck in my healing journey, unable to move beyond my agony. Looking back, I now wonder if this was because I carried an aspect of Judas that needed restoration—one that traditional healers, lacking the framework to understand such a connection, were unable to address.

Accessing my heart
As I reached out for help, it seemed like most people couldn't put a dent into the agony I was living with. I had so many years of struggle with seemingly no real reprieve or transformation. I sought out endless healers, spent a ton of money, and felt like I was barely making any movement forward.

Then in my early 30s, my physical health was falling apart. I herniated four disks in my back and was told that I would never be able to bend over and tie my shoes again. At the same time, I was extremely hyperthyroid. The endocrinologist I was working with told me the only option was to get rid of my thyroid: I could either have it removed via surgery or have it zapped with radioactive iodine. Either way, the thyroid had to go, and it was recommended that I live on medications for the rest of my life. Both of these situations led me right into the world of alternative healing because the mainstream was telling me that healing wasn't an option. It was my physical health that opened this door to the alternative realm. I just couldn't believe I couldn't heal, so I set out on a quest to find people that believed in our abilities to heal.

In my narrative, I continued to share my struggles with my back and my thyroid gland. It is fascinating to think about my thyroid condition as that gland represents speaking. If there was an aspect of Judas within my being, having my thyroid affected makes much sense. I end this section by stating, "*I set out on a quest to find people that believed in our abilities to heal.*" Was Judas questing, was he searching, via me, for people that genuinely believed he could heal? It is fascinating that I wrote that last sentence with the word 'our' instead of 'my': ... *so I set out on a quest to find people that believed in OUR abilities to heal.*

I moved on to share about different ways I had framed my story over the years. There were a few examples, but for the purpose of this book, I will list only this one:

The framework of a sensitive empath

For many years I jumped on the wagon that equated being a sensitive empath with someone that had no energetic boundaries; someone who didn't know where I ended, and someone else began; someone that could easily be destabilized by feeling the feelings of others; one that could not sense what is mine and what belongs to other people; ultimately a victim of other's emotional pain.

Are these experiences much broader than being empathic? I continued to share about feeling responsible for dealing with energies that entered my field. Was I writing about my experience with Judas before I consciously knew of our connection?

I wondered when energies entered my field if it was somehow my responsibility to deal with them. I wondered if I had signed up to transmute energies that would enter into my system. I grappled with the ethics of healing on other people's behalf because wouldn't I be taking away their soul development if I was doing their healing? Do I even have permission from someone else to heal their sorrows? Is not everyone standing in their free will to suffer as they choose...

How do I frame being sensitive? Am I defective or talented? Am I too sensitive or sophisticated in feeling energies? Today, when I feel others, I receive it as information in the form of vibrational frequencies. I note to myself; this is how their pain feels in my system. I don't declare that I know how they feel as I am feeling it through my nervous system, emotional body, and ultimately through my own filter. I take this information as a way to empathize with others, as a way to know more accurately how to pray for them. I take this energy I receive and send it out as a prayer. If it lingers around, I check in with how their story resonates with mine and see if being in their presence has triggered something in me that is calling for attention, calling to be healed.

Ultimately, my goal is to maintain a strong sense of self and a knowing of who I am even within the complexities of energies, including the collective consciousness. I choose to learn how to be a sophisticated empath versus a destabilized empath. While listening to others, I work on remaining open, receptive, compassionate, sensitive as well as grounded, and stabilized at the same time.

My contemplation about what to do when energies entered my field and if I am somehow responsible equally applies to carrying a fragment / aspect of Judas as it does to being empathic. My goal to maintain a strong sense of self and a knowing of who I am feels extra significant within the context of working with Judas in such an intertwined manner.

I titled the next section of my narrative, **"Knowing God as Medicine."**

As I continued on my journey, my relationship with the Divine was transforming. At one point in my journey, I was struggling with a skin rash. It was hot, red, inflamed, and painful. The rash felt like a hair coat, a self-punishment. To get rid of it, I tried everything, so I thought. I tried herbs, creams, changing my diet, soaking in baths. In telling my friends about this, one of them commented, "There are some things you haven't tried." I looked at him with a blank stare. He then asked, "Have you tried God? Have you tried love?"

I had not. I tried every way I could to be a war with this rash, to conquer it. It reminded me of when I was a child and had a sunburn - my skin was lobster red. I forced myself to take a hot bath, thinking that would be helpful. My mom informed me afterward that taking a cold bath would have been better as it would have cooled my skin. This was an epiphany. I had always thought of medicine as being painful. I did not know love as medicine; I did not know God as medicine.

As I was approaching God more and more, I realized that I had a PTSD response to God. In meditations, I would be melting into and merging with spaciousness, and then come to full alertness with a hyper-vigilance to my surroundings. What is included in all-there-is? Is the everything-ness, the spaciousness of the universe, and the Divine safe to experience?

I realized there is a profound difference between the Divine and humanity's construct of God. I realized I had been well indoctrinated into the constructs that God was vengeful, and hell was an op-

tion. I can see now that this wasn't true; it was indoctrination and the promotion of separation. Separation was good within the context of a wrathful God. It is good not to be so close and to keep a safe distance from such a being.

As the construct of a wrathful God was dissipating, I started to experience a different Creator, a loving Mystery. Yet, now that God is a loving Creator, I realized how much I felt that I was unworthy of Divine love. I didn't need to think about receiving God's love when God wasn't loving. But now that he is not a he and that Creator is Mysterious Loving Presence, I discovered that I believed I was unlovable and unworthy of love. I had tried to kill myself twice, and I had aborted a baby. If I had dishonored life, why would the Creator of life love me? Am I worthy of love? Am I worthy of life?

The more I opened to Creator's love, the more I realized I was mad as hell at Creator - livid for my entire life experience. Allowing myself to receive love from a being I was angry with was difficult... I also had this life-long feeling (outside of any context or any particular life events) that I had done something so wrong. So, the more I opened to Creator, the more I could really feel my belief of being unworthy of love, but also my belief that I am deserving of punishment. In the presence of a loving Creator, I felt I needed to atone for my existence: I am not worthy. I deserve to be punished. Therefore, I will not allow God to love me, forgive me, and support me (as if I have any say over what God does and doesn't do).

Could my life experiences have been shaped by a fragment of Judas—one that needed to make peace with God after enduring immense suffering for carrying out Jesus' request? Or was I carrying the imprint of others' belief that he had done something "so wrong"? I believe we can lose sight of our own truth and, instead, adopt the narratives others impose on us.

The next section, titled *"From Judas to Lazarus,"* explores my initial dreams of Judas, which I shared in Part 2 of this book.

> *During this time, I found myself thinking about Lazarus. To me, the archetype of Lazarus is that of awakening from the dead – not physical death, but awaking from a deadened heart, a deadened connection to God. It is an archetype of stepping back into life; an opportunity to live and to live more vibrantly; an opportunity to love; it is listening to the call of Creator.*
>
> *I feel Creator has always been calling; yet, I wasn't always able to hear. My heart was closed off to listening. The more I open my heart to listening, the more I hear Creator's call. I feel Creator called me back from the dead. Over the years, I have heard Creator's call in different ways. One such calling was in my late 20s after my second suicide attempt. Upon healing, I had a calling to become a nun. I was very confused by this as I left the church and Jesus many years ago. The thought, "I want to be a nun," was so persistent and invasive that I found myself in a Catholic church asking a Sister of Mercy if there was someone I could talk to about*

> *this. Long story short, I discerned religious life for a year, and then one day, I knew this part of my journey was complete. I understood Jesus had called me back. The pendulum needed to swing from one extreme (throwing Jesus out of my life) to the other (religious life) so that it may be cen-tered on the path as needed....*

Was Creator calling both Judas and me? Why the pull toward religious life? Did I need to repair my relationship with Jesus in order to align with my role in helping Judas? Did I need to walk the path of the middle?

> *I feel Creator reaching out in other ways as well. One day, I was at a friend's home, and she asked what sparrows meant to me. She was asking me because right before I arrived, a bird had flown into the window. When she went out to find the bird to see if it was okay, she didn't see one, so she went back inside. Then a sparrow got stuck between the glass door and the screen. As she helped release it, the bird flew off without any issue.*
>
> *To me, Creator speaks through creation, so when she asked, what sparrows mean to me, I burst into tears. In the bible, there is a passage about all sparrows being taken care of by the Father. For so long, I felt I was living proof that this was not true as I was the one and only forgotten sparrow. A sparrow's presence reminds me of Creator's love. Legend has it that sparrows were the only birds present throughout the crucifixion of Jesus; they are a symbol of awakening to a new life, of over-coming death. They represent dignity, self-worth,*

> *being worthy of God's love. They represent freedom (life) from oppression (death).*
>
> *I continue to feel called to step more and more into a vibrant, connected life—a life of flow and love. I continue to remain open to learning how to connect with Creator; to heal aspects of myself that believe I am separate from Creator and all that is; to allow Creator to infuse my thinking, my emotions, my behaviors, and every cell of my body; to see all life (including my own) as an expression of consciousness.*

While rereading my narrative, I wondered if Judas and I have been lifelong companions without me even knowing it. As I grew and changed over the years, was there a subsequent healing of the fragment I carried; as I sorted out my relationship with God, was there a corresponding healing for Judas on any level of his being?

The next section in my narrative was titled, **"From empathy to oneness: I am the other"**

> *I was exercising at the gym one day. A man was next to me on the elliptical. I had seen this man a few times before, and he was a chatty one, one that complained, one that carried his physical struggles like badges of honor. I tried to maintain my space from him... Yet, one morning, we wound up on ellipticals right next to each other. In a moment of surrender, in a moment of being open to loving him, rather than judging him, in a moment of putting aside my fear of getting sucked into his drama, in a moment of being open, I felt myself as*

> him. I felt myself over six feet tall, with physical injuries that I was recovering from. I felt past surgeries I never had as "Kerry." I felt what it was like to have his body, to move as he moved.
>
> I wasn't attempting to empathize. I wasn't attempting to feel his pain. I was simply trying not to be fearful and judgmental. I was trying to open to another experience, and in opening, I opened myself to sensing a part of his experience for a few moments. I looked over at him and felt I was him... in this moment, there was no other. In this moment, I knew myself. I am the daughter and the father. I am the sister and the mother. I was this man in a large, disabled, wounded body. Most striking to me was: I am the victim and my victors. I am my perpetrator. I am the opposite of all I think I am... I am the good I cannot see in myself. I am the bad that I see in others...

This experience feels akin to carrying a soul fragment of Judas. It reminds me of journeys where I embodied Judas, fully inhabiting his large physical form. It also echoes my experiences with the infinity symbol—moments of merging with all of existence, where I became both Judas and *'The Mother'* simultaneously.

The final section of my narrative was titled, **"Doing my best to live intentionally."**

> I continue to journey forward in my life and strive to make choices that are for my highest good. Yet, for me, the real question is not about what choices I want to make in my life; it is about how do I gain

access to the choices I wish to make in my life? How do I gain access to the ability to be, feel, think, and relate as I truly desire? How do I gain the ability and the capacity to choose thoughts, choose emotions, choose behaviors and live intentionally? How do I migrate from unconscious patterns to conscious choices?

In certain areas of my life, I have experienced a profound inability to move forward, overcome a behavior, change a thought pattern, and manifest certain work opportunities. In certain areas, I do not experience, "The world is my oyster," and I can manifest whatever my heart desires. In certain times in my life, I have experienced, "The world is my oyster, and my shell is not opening. Fantastic that I have a shell, but it is not opening." To me, there is a distinction between having choices and having the ability to access and act upon that choice and live intentionally. When I cannot access and act upon a choice, I explore where I may be hooked, where I may be stuck, where I may be swimming in the collective consciousness, where I may be drowning in my subconsciousness, where I may be tethered to ancestral patterns alive in my DNA, where I might be imprinted from a parallel or past life that is having a strong influence on this life.....

Much of my journey in moving forward has been to include the multidimensionality of my being. I used to believe that it was only past, unresolved traumas that led to the inability to choose that which I was consciously desiring. The key to overcoming

> *real stagnation, paralysis in certain areas, including lifelong issues, has been to energetically find and transform the entanglement, be it ancestral patterns, soul fragments from others in my field, my soul being fragmented, being connected to mass consciousness, imprints from past / parallel lives,...*

I chucked when I reread this section and noticed that I actually mention *"soul fragments from others in my field."* Before I became aware of my connection to Judas, was I unconsciously navigating my experience with him; sensing something I could not consciously name?

> *My journey towards access to choice has not been through asking Creator to unlock the doors of the prison and hand me what I want but asking Creator for the strength to be with what is. I pray, "Be with me as I am baffled as to why I am still here struggling with a lifelong pattern. Help me access that which I am entangled in by feeling my way through the vibrational essence. Be with me as I enter the chambers of my heart and dismantle the unconscious pattern by digesting the emotions of the past experiences, from whatever timeframe....*

> *There is something so powerful about bringing that which is festering and growing inside of me out into the light and having someone else listen and witness my journey. There is something about spelling it out to someone that dis-spells and diffuses the energy of an issue or a pattern. I feel that a big part of my healing has been breaking the spell that I have been under - a hypnotic spell. This*

> *spell stayed in place because there was so much shame in sharing my truth. With my story kept inside, this spell had me locked in place. When my horrors were kept in darkness, they had power over me. The more I bring my struggles to the light, the more they dissipate. In sharing my story - in spelling out my story - the spell continues to break, and I gain more and more freedom from my own history.*

The language of 'breaking spells' and 'horrors kept in the dark' makes me wonder: Was this ever just about me? Or was this about Judas too—about telling his story truthfully, breaking the spell of deception, and bringing his truth into the light?

> *It brings this sense of "Was that really me; my life?" as if I am sharing about another person's journey when telling my story. Some shifts in my life have led me to feel that my past was not even mine or that it was another lifetime.*

This feeling—that my past was not entirely my own—resounds deeply with my connection to Judas. I close my narrative by sharing:

> *I have been able to transform my relationship with God. Augustine of Hippo wrote, "To fall in love with God is the greatest of romances..." There are many romance stories, yet for me, falling in love with life, with God, and with all of creation has been the greatest of all romances. Living in this timeless ro-*

mance with God is my love story. Romance is a relationship, and deepening my romance with God is my life...

Albert Einstein said, "I think the most important decision we make is whether we believe we live in a friendly or hostile universe." One of the most important decisions I have made is to believe we live in a friendly Universe with a loving Creator. I choose friendly. I choose to be a loved, supported, unforgotten sparrow. I choose love and being loved. Additional choices I have made in my life are to not to claim my story from a place of victimhood - but rather from my soul's yearning to learn; and the choice to be curious, rather than judgmental, about my inability to choose certain things with grace and ease. These have been some of the most loving choices I have made for myself.

The ability to choose love is the greatest gift I have ever received.

It fascinates me how my narrative unfolded as it did. As I mentioned before, I wrote my story after my initial dreams of Judas but before my 2018 journeys, where I saw the fragment I carried being returned to him. Did my way of telling my story allow the energy of his fragment to find expression? I wonder if my narrative serves as a window into that fragment—perhaps even offering insight into aspects of Judas's own life and death.

My love for Judas runs deep. If some of my life experiences were indeed shaped by the imprint of his fragment, I would walk this path again—without hesitation. I am profoundly grateful for Judas, and I would willingly undertake this journey as a carrier all over again. I believe there was a mutual agreement between us, and not only do I reject any sense of victimhood, but I feel truly honored to have worked with him in this way. I am deeply moved that he trusted me with this mission, and I pray that I fulfill my responsibilities.

Works Cited

Brakke, D. (2015). Gnosticism: From Nag Hammadi to the Gospel of Judas. Course Guidebook. Virginia: The Teaching Company

Brown, M. (date). THE CHAMELEON MIRROR: From Integrating Emotion to Awakening Felt Perception. A Companion for THE PRESENCE PROCESS. https://www.thepresenceprocessportal.com/the-chameleon-mirrir.php

Ehrman, B. D. (2006). The Lost Gospel of Judas Iscariot: A New Look at Betrayer and Betrayed. [PDF]. New York: Oxford University Press, Inc.

Kasser, R., Meyer, M., & Wurst, G. (2008). The Gospel of Judas. Washington, D.C.: National Geographic Society

Meyer, M. (2007). Judas: The Definitive Collection of Gospels and Legends About the Infamous Apostle of Jesus. New York: HarperCollins Publishers

Pagels, E. H., & King, K. L. (2008). Reading Judas: The Gospel of Judas and the shaping of Christianity. England: Penguin Books

Gospel of Judas passages quoted in this book come from the translation done by Rodolphe Kasser, Marvin Meyer, and Gregor Wurst, in collaboration with François Gaudard. From: The Gospel of Judas. ©2006 by The National Geographic Society

Biblical passages quoted in this book are from Holy Bible, New International Version, NIV ©2011 by Biblica, Inc.

About the Author

Kerry Jehanne-Guadalupe

Kerry Jehanne-Guadalupe is a transformative guide in the healing arts, dedicated to supporting individuals and communities to unlock deep healing and authentic self-expression. As a channel of light language, her work is enriched by years of study in energy healing, emotional resilience, and mind-body modalities, including HeartMath, Emotional Freedom Techniques, and Transformational Breath. Over the span of 15 years, Kerry has facilitated many wellness-related workshops, including Light Language Transmissions, "Dancing with the Beloved: A Workshop in Conscious Partnership," Empathy, Conflict Resolution, and more.

As a light language practitioner, Kerry's healing work extends beyond individual sessions—she has led light language workshops to support those affected by global crises and offered live transmissions for collective healing. Kerry's albums of light language, *Illumination*, and *Rising*, available through streaming platforms, are immersive journeys within the medicinal nature of light language.

A passionate writer and educator, Kerry explores consciousness, wellness, and transformation through her blog *Elevated Existence*, and published books, including *Optimizing Existence*, *The Mystery of Judas*, *The Devil's Yoga*, co-editor of and chapter contributor in *Pathways of Intentionality*. Through her writing, she delves into the intricate connections between belief systems, emotions, personal power, and transcendence, often challenging conventional narratives. Kerry has given numerous book talks and has been featured in podcasts, interviews, and media discussions on holistic well-being.

Kerry's diverse background includes organic farming, beekeeping, as well as adult education within academia and organizations. She holds a master's in Adult and Extension Education from Cornell University. She has served as an adjunct professor and a farm-based educator, highlighting her commitment to sustainability, community wellness, and personal empowerment. Kerry is on the board of *Relationships with Purpose*, a 501(c) 3 organization servicing unhoused individuals in Sacramento, California, and is the co-founder of a new and private publishing company, *Journey of the Phoenix*.

Website: www.kerryjehanne.com
Light Language: https://www.youtube.com/@KerryJehanne
Medium: https://medium.com/@kerryjehanne

Made in the USA
Coppell, TX
16 April 2025

48381192R10142